Investing
for the
Long-Term

Robert Linggard

TTL is an imprint of
Take That Ltd.
P.O.Box 200
Harrogate
HG1 2YR
ENGLAND

email:sales@takethat.co.uk

www.takethat.co.uk

TTL are always keen to receive ideas and manuscripts for new financial books. Please send details to the address above.

ISBN 1-873668-76-7

Take That Ltd. books are available at special quantity discounts to use as premiums and sales promotions, or for use in corporate training programs. For more information, please contact the Director of Special Sales at the above address or contact your local bookshop.

CONTENTS

Preface 5

1. Introduction and some Moral Justification 7

2. The Asset Markets 28

3. Buying and Selling Stocks and Shares:
   How the markets work 50

4. Past and Present Masters 64

5. Wise Investing 79

6. Reading Company Accounts 104

7. Financial Information:
   Finding it and using it. 123

8. Misfortunes, Mistakes, and Deliberate Fraud:
   What to do when things go wrong 138

9. Money, Banks and the Business Cycle. 153

10. A Wider, Deeper, Longer Term View 172

Dedication:

This book is dedicated to my wife, Margaret, and my two children, Nick and Nadine.

Preface

It would be very satisfying to say that the investment techniques described in this book have made me a very rich man, but that would not be true. Over decades of investing, I searched long and hard to for a method of investing that was both secure and successful. It took me a long time to find it, and only in the last few years have I managed to establish the confidence and discipline necessary to invest wisely on a long term basis.

When I began investing I had beginner's luck. In the long run this turned out to be a mixed blessing. While it inspired me to get more deeply involved, it also gave me the impression that investing profitably was quite easy. When my luck ran out, I not only lost money, but confidence as well, and it was only with misfortune that I realised that the task I had set myself was considerably harder than I had ever imagined.

The opinions I express throughout are my own. The system of investing I propose is a simplified version of methods used by the great investors mentioned in chapter four. The whole book is designed for people who have only a limited amount of time to spend analysing stocks and shares, and yet wish to control their own investment portfolio. I believe that this can be done successfully by the average person, with a little care and regular attention.

Robert Linggard.
bobling@paston.co.uk

Chapter One

Introduction and some Moral Justification

Saving for Old Age

Since the beginning of civilisation, men and women have prepared for old age by having large families. Bringing up a family was like saving for a pension and children were the 'capital' that a man and his wife built up during their working lives. Healthy children took the place of a healthy saving account. They were fed, clothed, educated, often with difficulty, though usually with loving care. In the fullness of time, it was these children who would provide care for their parents when they grew too old to work.

The custom was, that as the parents grew older, their children would gradually take over running of the family farm or business. Sometimes this would result in three of four generations living in the same house in what we now call an 'extended' family, but which for them was simply family. Even though the parents retained ownership, the children were the effective managers.

A modern economist would probably argue that the care the parents received was the 'dividend' paid by the children for the use of their parents 'capital'. However, this would be imposing a modern explanation on a very ancient custom.

The extended family with its system of care has been a fact of life for countless generations of peasant farmers, in Europe and throughout the world for at least ten thousand years. Even today, this is still the situation in many third world countries, and it is one of the main causes of over-population, as it was in Europe until recent times. Having a large family is like having a large pension and health-care insurance combined.

The human species is unique in this behaviour. Although other animals care for their young, they do so only until the young animals are old enough to feed themselves. No other species cares for its elderly parents. The custom of parents looking after their children up to their teenage years, and that of children caring for their parents in old age, is one of the main reasons why the family has been the basic unit of human society for thousands of years.

Other social systems with communal raising of children and caring for the elderly have always broken down after one or two generations. 'Communism' in this simple sense doesn't seem to work. Family units are remarkably stable, and loyalty to family seems, on average, to be stronger than loyalty to any other kind of organisation. The stability of society has depended, until recently, on the custom that children have parents to provide for them when they are young, and parents have children to take care of them when they are old. Thus, privilege and responsibility go hand in hand.

Extended family care has been our tradition for thousands of years. However, in modern western civilisation this system is giving way to a different way of life, and the majority of the population no longer live in extended families. The state is increasingly taking over the care of children, especially their education. Quite often now, it intervenes to remove children from parental care if that care falls below a certain standard. But more importantly, all citizens are now entitled to a state pension when they are old and do not need to rely on their children for care.

The vast majority of children now leave the home of their parents to make homes for themselves, even before they marry. Very few children, these days, take over the business interests of their parents, they much prefer to choose a career which suits their own abilities and ambitions. Elderly parents are now expected to take care of themselves or to purchase whatever care they need if the state cannot provide it. Of course, many people still support their elderly parents with love and care, if not with money, but it is no longer the social obligation that is used to be.

In an industrial state, the debt to one generation from the next, has been more or less 'communalised'. The money we save for our old age via pension schemes is invested. These investments are used to build new industries and new facilities for more efficient living. It is the children we have raised who will work in these new industries and facilities, and the profits from them will provide the income we receive from our pension investments. The elder generation is still cared for by the younger one, but on a national basis rather than in extended family units.

The socialist dogma that profit is immoral is seriously narrow-minded. Profit is both the consequence of investment and its motivation. It was the reason why, in the past, people had large families, and it is the reason why, now, we save in pension schemes. The modern system is better because it provides choice and it averages out the effects of accidents and family disasters.

The socialist ideal of communal care of children and old people has been advanced more by investment in pension schemes than by attempts at centralised control of production and distribution. The market economy may often be primitive and unfair, but the way forward is by improving its efficiency and fairness - not by abolishing it.

Saving: Cash versus Assets

In spite of its unfair distribution, money is, perhaps, the greatest benefit that civilisation has brought to mankind. It represents economic choice, and in as much as choice may be identified with freedom, it is the foundation stone of a free society. From our own personal point of view, the only thing wrong with money is that we don't have enough of it. However, no government, since the Bolshevik revolution in 1917, has tried to get rid of it. And even the stubborn Bolsheviks eventually had to accept it as an essential part of a modern civilised state.

Money first came into use about 3000 years ago, and ever since then, prudent men and women have saved it. Traditionally, saving money simply meant not spending it, but now, with the advent of bank savings' accounts, money saved is really money invested, if not by you, then by the bank you are saving with.

In the days when money was metallic, that is gold, silver, and copper coins, saving was a sensible thing to do because money almost always maintained its value. Sometimes, in recessions, money even increased in purchasing power. The hoards of coins which are found periodically, hidden in old houses or buried in the ground, are usually the lost savings of former generations. They are always worth more today than when they were first hidden, not only for the rarity value of the coins, but also for the metallic value of the gold or silver they are made from.

Until this century, even paper money in Europe and America was based on gold or silver. In England the unit of currency is the pound sterling, based originally on one pound weight of silver in Anglo-Saxon times. Silver only gave way to the golden guinea in the eighteenth century, which was itself replaced by the gold sovereign in the nineteenth century.

A pound weight of silver is a very large amount of money. But the advantage of metal money is that it can be sub-divided into smaller units or coins. If necessary, these can always be recombined into bullion simply by melting. In the long history of the silver pound, it has been coined into pennies, shillings, crowns, half crowns, six-penny pieces, groats and three-penny bits. Though the purity and value of these coins have varied considerably, the pound Sterling was the solid basis of our currency for about 1000 years until the early eighteenth century.

Long term investment

It is interesting to calculate how profitable it would have been to save metallic money of this kind over such a long period. Imagine that we had a medieval ancestor who, in the year 1100, had hidden one hundred pounds in silver coins for us to find in the year 2000. Discounting the rarity value of the coins, the value of 100 pounds weight of silver, at today's price of about £4 per ounce, is approximately £6,400. A sum well worth having but not a very good return for nine hundred years of hoarding.

In fact the increase by a factor of 64 is equivalent to a compound interest rate of less than 0.5% per year. This is less than the historic rate of inflation, which over 900 years, averages out at about 0.7% per annum.

However, most of this inflation has occurred in the present century. For over 800 years the average rate of inflation was only about 0.5% per annum. So hoarding coins would have been worthwhile until about 1914. After that date, the ravages of twentieth century inflation have consistently made it more profitable to put your money in a bank rather than to save coins.

It seems obvious to us that our ancient ancestor could have done more with his £100 than just saving the money as silver coins. However, if we consider what options he had, we begin to understand why so much coin was hoarded. Investing in shares was not possible since joint stock companies did not develop until the sixteenth century. Putting the money on deposit in a bank was not possible since public banks weren't invented until the seventeenth century. Neither did the monarchs of the day issue secure government bonds with an attractive interest rate. That did not begin until the eighteenth century. In 1100, the only safe alternative to hoarding cash was to buy land.

The Doomsday Book, compiled by the King's Commissioners in 1086, is a valuation of all the property in England, and this consisted almost entirely of agricultural land. For example, the village of Ogbourne in Wiltshire, was valued at £25. The area of land was recorded as 30 Hides, about 3000 acres by modern measures. With recent agricultural land values of about £2,000 per acre, the £25 valuation would now have grown to £6 million, and £100 invested in land in 1100 would now be worth about £24 million. The growth factor is now 240,000, which is a compound interest rate of 1.4%. Not really outstanding but at least it is better than inflation, and a lot better than hoarding coin.

Inflation

From Roman times onwards, the supply of precious metals for coinage in Europe was always inadequate. The amount of money in circulation was always too little to support the economic activity of a growing population. This was one of the reasons why, from medieval times to the reformation, high unemployment was the normal state of the economy. The limited supplies of gold and silver resulted in money tending to retain its value, that is, there was little or no inflation, and in some years, prices actually fell.

Figure 1 indicates how the price of goods has inflated since medieval times. The graph shows the average price of a set amount of goods, costing £1 in 1100. We see that it was more or less stable for four hundred years. During this period the majority of the population were peasant farmers, and produced for themselves almost all the things that they needed. The blip in the middle of the 1300's is the disruption caused by the Black Death, in which almost 30% of the population of Europe died.

At the beginning of the reformation, around 1500, there is a surge in inflation. This was due mainly to the large amounts of gold and silver that began to flood into Europe from the newly discovered continent of America. In England, this increase in the amount of money was augmented by the dissolution of the monasteries, when gold and silver plate were melted down for coinage. In addition, the sale of abbey lands returned savings back into circulation.

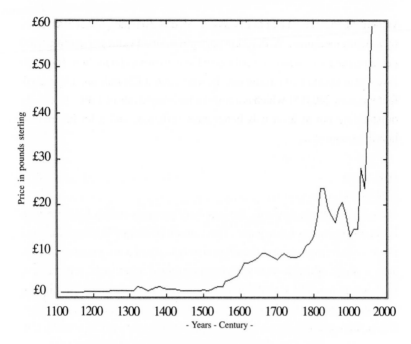

Figure 1: Inflation Since Medieval Times

After this surge in inflation, prices were again stable until the middle of the 1700's when the British government began borrowing heavily to finance European wars. By this time banking was developing rapidly and bank credit permitted an excess of government spending. The surge in inflation peaked in the early 1800s, after Napoleon was defeated. For a while the banks could not redeem notes with gold coins, but gradually, the situation righted itself and gold was restored at its former value.

The really big jump in inflation coincides with the first world war, when again, the government borrowed on a massive scale to finance the war effort. Again, in doing so, it was forced to abandon the gold standard. This time however, there was no going back. An attempt to do so was a part cause of the great depression of the 1930's during which prices fell back again, almost to pre-war levels.

13

The advent of the second world war again brought inflation, as might be expected. After this war prices did not fall, though they did stabilise for a few years. However, by the 1960's many factors contributed to a massive increase in money supply, and inflation rose more rapidly than at any other time in our history.

Hyper-inflation

Once money is divorced from the value of silver or gold, the phenomena of rampant inflation becomes possible. Once money can be created at will in the form of bank notes or bank deposits, the amount of money in circulation can be increased without limit. In times of war and other emergencies, governments often decide to permit the money supply to increase rather than to impose tax increases or to raise interest rates. Thus, the amount of goods or services that can be bought by a unit of currency, diminishes as more money floods into circulation. In such circumstances, saving money is not a wise thing to do.

When the gold standard was abandoned, gold coins disappeared from circulation and were replaced by paper bank notes. Figure 2 shows the progress of inflation since 1914 – where the adjective 'rampant' is clearly merited. The chart shows the 'retail price index' a measure of inflation introduced in 1914. In the twentieth century, the value of the pound declined by a factor of 54. This is more than five times the amount it had inflated in the previous eight hundred years. However, in a historical context, the pound Sterling is one of the world's most stable currencies.

Consider the German mark and the decline in its value during the period 1920 to 1923. After the defeat of the first world war, the German government attempted to solve its balance of payments difficulties by printing more and more money. In January 1921 the exchange rate was about 65 marks for one dollar. By November 1923, the exchange rate was 4,200 billion marks to the dollar. Just to make this clear, written in full, the ratio was 4,200,000,000,000 to 1.

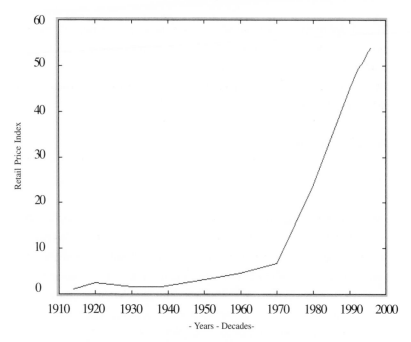

Figure 2: The Progress of inflation since 1914

The word used for this phenomenon was 'hyper-inflation'. Any one with savings in bank deposits effectively lost them. During this period, there was a rush to buy assets, any assets, rather than hold onto money. Of course, the demand for things to buy pushed up their price, which is the very definition of inflation. The lesson here is that once inflation reaches a critical level, the rush to buy assets will cause it to get worse. In that event, money becomes worthless so quickly that people buy anything which in the future they can barter for the goods they need. It is perhaps after this experience of economic disaster that German investors became so famously conservative.

Bank Deposits

It is not surprising that the hoarding of bank notes is almost completely unheard of. Not only is paper currency notoriously perishable, but it is also likely to be rendered valueless by changes in the design of the notes. Fortunately, we can save money in almost perfect security by placing it in a bank deposit account. Literally, 'deposit' means that the bank takes our money, and physically 'deposits' it in its vaults, which is what used to be done in the banks of the early 1600's. Of course, today no such thing happens, the bank merely makes a record that we have given it a certain sum of money. When we ask for it to be returned, we do not receive the same bank notes we originally deposited, but others of appropriate design and value.

Another great benefit of owning money as bank deposits, is that the bank will pay interest on the amount deposited. Since the bank is in the business of lending money, it is willing to pay to acquire money as bank deposits. In effect we lend our money to the bank. So, unlike hoarded gold coins, bank deposits of money grow over the years as the interest mounts up.

Unfortunately, the interest on bank deposits varies from time to time in relation to the rate of inflation. High interest rates are associated with high rates of inflation, so that the more interest we get on our savings deposits, the greater the rate at which our savings lose their real value. It is a sad fact, that no matter how fast our savings grow due to the interest paid, their real value, in terms of the goods and services they can buy, grows at a much slower rate, if at all. For several years during the last half century, the rate of inflation has actually exceeded bank interest rates, that is, savings have lost real value.

The solution to this dilemma is to buy assets. That is, things that we can sell for money at some future date. Our hope is that the assets we buy will also increase in price, hopefully, faster than the rate of inflation. This way we gain more by buying assets than we would by keeping our savings in bank deposits. It is, therefore, very important to buy the right kind of assets, and the main purpose of this book is explain exactly how this can be done.

Property

Assets, by definition, are things which people regard as being of value. We have already seen that land did much better than coins over a period of nine hundred years. This is still true today, buildings and the land on which they stand, usually called 'property', are a solid investment in both senses of the word. For the generations since the first world war, one of the main ways for ordinary people to accumulate assets has been house purchase via a mortgage. This not only eliminates the need to pay rent, but provides a very secure way of saving - you actually live in your investment.

Since the 1920s, the increase in population has ensured a steady rise in the price of houses over and above inflation. For that reason, buying a house with a mortgage was a good way for a man and his wife to save and invest. After paying off the mortgage over their working lives, the couple became, on retirement, the owners of a valuable asset.

By moving to a smaller, less expensive, house, they could release some of this capital to augment their pension. Traditionally, they put this money into a building society deposit account from which they received interest. Thus, young couples buying their first house allow the older couples to realise some of their assets. In addition, the younger people paying interest on their mortgages, provide the interest that the older generation receives on its building society savings. Again we see the phenomenon of the younger generation providing for their elders

Joint Stock Companies

Property is not now the main source of wealth for individuals or for the country as a whole. Land and the food it produces represent a very small part of the productive capacity of any industrialised nation. Manufacturing and service industries account for almost all of the economic activity in an industrial state. It is the ownership of these industries which constitutes the main part of its citizens' wealth. These assets are held in the form of shares, and shares in companies are a very special kind of asset.

The history of share owning goes back to the days of sea-going merchants. They risked their capital and often their lives to trade goods in foreign lands. Sailing with a cargo of valuable merchandise on dangerous seas, often made more hazardous by the activities of pirates, was a risky business. The risks of these ventures were often shared amongst a group of business men. If the ship was lost then the loss was shared, and no one was completely ruined as a result. If the ship came home, then the profit was shared by all participants in the enterprise.

The idea of sharing risk and profit originated in Italy in the twelfth century. A contract called a 'contratto di commenda' was drawn up between the merchant and his backers to share the costs and the profits of the enterprise. This format was copied all over Europe, making its way from Italy via Germany, France, Spain and the Netherlands to England. This principle of sharing risk was extended to land-based enterprises, for example, building a water mill, or draining land for agriculture. The advantage of this arrangement was not just that the risk was shared, but that much larger projects were made possible because the number of people involved could be increased indefinitely.

During the industrial revolution, companies hoping to make money out of new inventions multiplied many-fold. It was only natural that some of these projects would fail, and partners in failed companies sometimes found themselves in the position of having to find additional money to pay off the company's debts. It was this problem that led to the creation of the Limited Liability Company.

In the Companies Act of 1862, the legal form of the limited liability company was defined. This important law was an attempt to ameliorate the disadvantages of unlimited liability, whilst retaining the advantages of risk and profit sharing. The modern form of this law is to be found in the 1986

Companies Act which defines the difference between a private company and a public company.

The companies whose shares are traded on the London Stock Exchange are Public Limited Companies, known as Plc's. Any company which does not have PLC after its name must be assumed to be a private company. Essentially, a public limited company is a fictitious person, rather like the merchant in the old days, who can take on debts and be held responsible for them. However, if the company becomes bankrupt, this fictitious person conveniently dies, and the debts do not devolve on the owners of the company.

The advantages of owning shares are almost entirely limited to the privilege of receiving dividends.

As a part owner, a shareholder is not entitled, at any time, to demand to see the books or to talk to the managers. That privilege is restricted to the day of the company's annual general meeting, when the directors of the company must present the company accounts and report to the shareholders. They must also face questions from shareholders and subject themselves to re-appointment by vote. For the rest of the year, the directors and managers, not unreasonably, claim the right to be left alone to get on with the business of running the company.

Some companies give their shareholders certain 'perks' connected with the company's products. For example, cross-channel ferry companies used to give discounted fares to shareholders. But this practice is falling out of use as companies become more commercially minded and investors seek profits in the form of cash.

Today, the risks of owning shares are limited entirely to the loss of the money you paid for the shares themselves. However, this is risk enough for people who are investing their life's savings. So it is well to remember that even though buying a share is free from any financial liability, there is always a finite possibility that the company will go bust. No matter how big a company is, and how secure it might appear, that company can always go into loss, and eventually into bankruptcy.

For example, the conglomerate Poly Peck, was a large and important company valued at hundreds of millions of pounds. Yet, in less than a year, its shares lost almost all their value. This consideration leads many people to save via mutual Funds (collective schemes, either investment trust, or unit trusts), or to just leave it to managers of a pension fund.

Saving and Investing

The wealthy have always been able to save for their old age. So there is a tradition of saving and investing in the UK that goes back to the early 1700s.

Earlier this century, the government instituted compulsory national insurance, a scheme which was intended to provide every working person with a pension at the age of 65. This state pension is not paid from an investment fund, but from government revenues. In order to reduce future tax bills, recent governments have resisted demands to increase this pension in line with average earnings. Consequently, the social value of the state pension has steadily declined. This has led, in the past twenty years, to a large increase in the number of people saving and investing for old age.

The government encourages saving and investment by making a number of tax concessions available to savers and investors. The table right shows the taxation arrangements of seven different saving and investment schemes supported by the government.

There are three points at which the government has a right to impose tax. The main one is income tax you pay on the money you may want to save or invest. They can also take tax on the investment return, that is, the capital gain and income of the fund itself.

Scheme	Investment Decisions	Taxation	Pension
Company Pension	fund managers	not original income not on growth on final pension	fund itself
Private Pension	fund managers	not original income not on growth on final pension	annuity
SIPPS	yourself	not original income not on growth on final pension	annuity
PEP	yourself	on original income not on growth not on dividends	dividends
Private Portfolio	yourself	on original income on growth on dividends	dividends
ISAS	yourself	on original income not on growth on dividends	dividends

Finally, they can tax any subsequent income you receive as pension from an annuity purchased from your accumulated assets. (See chart above).

The tax concession on income paid into a pension fund has a penalty. When you retire the government does not trust you to use your pension assets as you wish. It insists that you effectively hand them over to an investment company who will then provide you with an annuity for the rest of your life. There is some wisdom in this. Children have a habit of needing large sums of money, especially when they know such sums are available. Parents, in their old age, are in no good position to resist such demands, and having the money invested beyond recall protects them from their own generous natures.

For private portfolios, PEPs and ISAs, your pension income is taken as dividends from your investments. That is, you make your own decisions about the kind of financial instruments you wish to buy to provide you with a pension income.

The disadvantage of this is that you take the risk of the investment failing and leaving you with reduced income. The advantage is that the capital remains in your possession to pass on to your children when you die. With an annuity, the capital becomes the property of the company which provides the annuity.

Pension Funds

The purchase of assets via a Pension Fund is the most important way in which people in a modern society save for their old age. Pension funds are collective saving and investment schemes. These investment funds receive regular contributions from members throughout their working lives and use them to purchase assets. From these assets they pay pensions to retired members.

The actual amount of the pension is related to the accumulated value of the contributions plus their growth. In a mature, company pension scheme, the contributions from active members are used first to pay the pensions of the retired members. The balance is then used to buy more assets for the fund. Again, we see a younger, working generation providing income for the older, retired generation.

As well as company pensions, there are private pension schemes which operate in a much the same way. To become entitled to a pension, it is necessary to make regular contributions to the fund over a period of many years. These contributions are used to buy assets, which both accumulate and grow in value. A private pension scheme works in the same way as a company pension scheme until the member retires. The private pension fund does not pay pensions directly. At the time of retirement, the contributor's accumulated assets are used to buy an annuity. Pension funds, both private and company, are controlled by government legislation, and pension funds are permitted to buy only a limited range of 'financial instruments'. The investments which pension law permits, are required to be low risk rather than high return. This is to reduce the risk of the fund falling in value. The permitted investments consist of bank deposits, property, stocks and shares of public companies, and government bonds.

Of course, the pension fund managers do not manage funds as an act of charity, they have to be paid, and they often require very high salaries. This means that pension funds charge management 'fees' which are related to the value of the fund rather than the amount of work involved, or the increase in the value of the fund. These fees are usually a small percentage of the fund's asset value. So, even if the fund does not make money, the managers still get their percentage.

It is the management cost of private pensions that has led many people to consider running their own pension fund. This can be done via a 'Self Invested Personal Pension Scheme' (SIPPS). This works in exactly the same way as other pension schemes except that the contributor is the sole and only member of the fund. He makes the investment decisions, and on retirement, he may use the accumulated assets to buy an annuity.

The tax concessions on income invested in a SIPPS pension, are exactly the same as for the other pension schemes. However, the contributor may not register the assets directly in his own name. The pension fund must be controlled by a trustee company licensed to do so by the government. These trustee companies charge a fixed annual fee, about £500, for this service. This is reasonable because it is independent of the asset value of the fund. If you have as little as £20,000 of assets in the fund, the fee is only

2.5%, a typical charge for a professional pension fund. The duty of the trustees is to see that you only invest in assets permitted to pension funds, bank deposits, government bonds, certain property, and shares in public companies. Otherwise, the trustee company will allow you to control your own pension fund investments, deciding when and what to buy and sell. This can make a big difference to the accumulated value of your pension when you come to retire. If you have been wise then it is possible to provide yourself with a pension larger than that you would have obtained from a private pension scheme.

Personal Portfolios

Of course, you don't have to be running your own pension fund to benefit from a wisely invested portfolio. Pension tax concessions are only available on a fraction of your income. Any other saving must be made out of taxed income and thus there is no need to put it into a pension scheme. To encourage people to build their own investment portfolios, the government set up the 'Personal Equity Plan'. This arrangement is similar to the SIPPS idea, except that there are no tax concessions on the money you put into it, and no requirement to buy an annuity. Furthermore, when you want to use the money as a pension, you can withdraw it as income without paying tax. More recently, PEPs have been replaced by Individual Saving Account Scheme (ISAs), which is not so generous on tax saving.

For a variety of reasons, more and more people are building their own investment portfolios, and reaping the rewards of increasing asset values. These people are finding that they want to have control of their own investments, their pension fund, or PEP, or ISA, or personal portfolio. Even where savings are already in the hands of a private pension company, it is possible for the individual to transfer his savings to a SIPPS fund. So the army of private investors is growing, and the facilities for them to obtain information and to trade stocks and shares are improving all the time.

The efficiency of buying and selling investments has improved many fold over the past twenty years. The actual cost of trading stocks and shares is constantly falling, especially with electronic share dealing. It is reaching the level at which it is no longer a significant factor when deciding whether to make changes in an investment portfolio. For new investors, the cost of building a personal portfolio is now less than the cost of buying into a unit trust or other mutual investment. The individual investor can take control of his own savings at a very moderate cost, and, providing they know which stocks and shares to buy, they can do at least as well as a professional fund.

This is, of course, the crucial issue, how does the private investor know which assets to invest in? Or to put it more dramatically, can the private investor beat the professional fund managers at their own game? The answer, surprisingly, is 'yes' because the private investor has one advantage that the professional does not have. Because his investments are small compared to those of a large collective fund, he can buy and sell stocks and shares without disturbing the price.

The manager of a large investment fund, with tens of million pounds invested in a single company's shares, cannot possibly sell the entire holding without the price falling significantly. Similarly, the fund manager cannot suddenly invest a significant proportion of the funds he manages in a single company without the share price rising considerably. So, although the professional has teams of expert analysts advising him which companies he should buy or sell, he can only do so if he accepts that the price of the shares will move against him as soon as he tries to execute his trading plan. Why, and to what extent, prices rise and fall as shares are in greater or lesser demand, is a feature of the market mechanism, which is discussed in the following chapters.

The principles of wise investing are easy to learn and only a little more difficult to practice. Over the years, the rules for identifying good companies whose shares are worth buying have been refined and tested. It is the purpose of this book to provide an intelligent guide to this kind of investment analysis, explaining as directly as possible how and why the rules work. In the process of doing this, it will be necessary to explain how companies work and how the investment industry, the major financial markers, and modern market economies operate.

We shall also discuss the problem of obtaining financial information, how to evaluate it, and in particular, how to read company accounts.

Finally, we shall look at the nature of money and banking, and the whole world economic system to identify the processes which cause booms and crashes. The objective is to do all this as simply and directly as possible, avoiding both jargon on the one hand, and over simplification on the other.

One final word

Despite modern technology, the world lives from hand to mouth. We cannot really 'save' the things we will need in old age. A house perhaps will last us for all the years of our retirement, but it will need many repairs in that time. Most of our clothes will need to be replaced on an annual basis, and the food we eat needs to be provided freshly every day. Some one has to do this for us, and it has to be the younger generation. They will look after us, not out of a sense of filial duty, but for sound economic reasons.

What we save is assets and to provide for ourselves in old age we need to sell these assets. Our system of saving and investment ensures that the savings of the younger generation is our income. This can only continue if there are enough young people willing to work and able to work and save. The security of our pensions lies not only in wise fund management but also in a stable social system. Additionally, since the savings of the younger generation pay our pensions, we have a vested interest in seeing that they are paid well enough to save some part of their income.

A major problem is that the facilities that enable people to save for old age are used to provide income for the children of the wealthy. The growing number of people who live in this way not only diverts resources from the older generation, but distract the younger generation from working and saving. The economic system we live in is by no means perfect, but it is efficient in ensuring that the young get educated and the old get taken care of. The future of civilisation lies in perfecting this system, not replacing it.

Chapter Two

The Asset Markets

Financial Instruments

Unlike our medieval ancestors, we now have a wide range of 'Financial Instruments' in which to invest our savings. A financial instrument is simply one of the many 'products' supplied by the so-called financial services 'industry'. They are essentially entitlements to some kind of financial benefit, because of this, they have value. As we shall see, this value is directly related to the level of this benefit and its reliability.

An important property of a financial instrument is that it can be bought and sold on a recognised and regulated financial market at a price, set more or less fairly, by the market mechanism. Below is a list of the ten most popular financial instruments used in the western economies.

- Building Society and Bank Savings Accounts
- British Government Bonds - gilts
- Bonds issued by Municipal Authorities and foreign governments
- Bonds issued by Public Companies
- Preference Shares in Public Companies
- Shares in Public Companies
- Options on Foreign Currencies
- Options on shares in public companies
- Futures Contracts in Foreign Currencies
- Futures Contracts in commodities and raw materials

These instruments are listed in order of security, that is, the most secure ones are listed first and the most risky at the end. The other parameter we are interested in is the 'return'. This is the money we gain from owning the instrument. Not surprisingly, risk and return are related in that the more return you go for, the greater the risk you will have to take. Return is usually expressed in percentage terms on an annual basis.

Unfortunately, there is no standard measure of risk. A financial instrument can only be said to be more or less risky than another instru-ment, but the risk is not usually expressed in numerical terms. As a basis for grading risk, an investment in British or American government bonds is traditionally regarded as being 'risk-free'. However, this does not mean that you will never lose money by buying them. Since bonds are bought and sold on a market, their price varies from day-to-day, and you cannot always sell for the same price that you paid to buy them

On the other hand, a bank deposit account will always return you at least as much money as you deposited in it. Because of the effects of inflation, the real value of your money may have fallen, but its numerical value will be the same or greater. The only way you can lose money deposited in a bank account is if the bank fails. This is a finite, though very small, risk. However, since there are now government protection schemes that compensate depositors in the event of bank failure, the risk of you losing your money in a bank is negligible.

Hence, in general, the safest place for your savings is in an account with a reputable bank or building society. This is one of the advantages that private investors have over large funds because investment funds are not so protected. However, it is well to note that deposit protection only applies up to a certain amount. So when you open an account it is wise to ask how much of your saving comes within the protection scheme. If you are very cautious, or 'risk-averse', you can spread your money around several banks and building societies.

Our medieval ancestor would be surprised to see that the above list does not even mention property and precious metals - the only two ways they had of investing for the future. In fact, neither is a good investment for the pension builder. Owning property directly is fraught with problems, and hoarding gold and silver coins is not recommended. We can still enjoy ownership of these two stalwarts, but it is better to do it via specialist companies.

Owning precious metals, as either coins or bullion, is a hazardous way of saving. Coins and ingots do not pay interest; in fact, you have to pay an annual fee for their safe-keeping. In addition, the value of gold and silver is now totally divorced from money, and it is subject to wide variations in price. Since they are no longer used as a basis for bank lending, no one is certain what their value should be. For those who feel that gold and silver are a good investment, it is much easier to own the metals via futures contracts, or to buy shares in the mining companies.

We have already seen how our wise medieval ancestor who bought land, did better over nine hundred years than any other investment that was available at that time. Land and buildings are almost always included as part of the fixed assets of a company. So, by owning company shares you also own property. However, some companies specialise in owning and managing property, that is, buildings and the land on which they stand.

By owning shares in a property company rather than by direct ownership, you can avoid the inconvenience of having to collect rents and organise building repairs. At the same time, the increase in the property's value will be reflected in the asset value of the shares, and the rents will still come to you in the form of dividends. Of course, many people own property directly and they derive an income from it, but this is in the nature of a business and it is not appropriate to discuss it here as an investment.

Each of these ten financial instruments has its own special properties, which makes it a useful component in an investment portfolio. The essential contrast is between risk and return; that is, the amount of return if the investment succeeds set against the risk that the investment will fail. As we shall see, the highest returns are available only from the riskiest instrument. Even though, ideally, we would like both high returns and great security for our investments, it will be necessary to make a compromise. This means making some difficult decisions. In fact, the whole art of wise investing is in making such decisions consistently well.

Bank and Building Society Accounts

In the UK, building societies have traditionally acted like banks which specialise in lending money for house purchase. Building societies have an excellent record of security. The fact that the money saved is lent for house purchase means that the assets behind the building society are very solid. In addition, the non-profit making status of the traditional building society has led to very prudent management of assets. However, many have recently been privatised, and the pressure to make profits will undoubtedly lead them to take more risks in their business.

Bank and building society accounts are the simplest of all methods of saving, yet in recent years new kinds of accounts have become available which need to be explained. Basically, you lend your money to a bank or building society, and they pay you interest. It used to be the case that the longer you were prepared to commit your money to them, the higher the rate of interest they would pay, known as 'term deposits'. Now, this relationship has all but disappeared, and high interest can be obtained even from a current account.

Banks and some building societies are profit making companies, and it is for their own benefit that they continually change the kinds of accounts they have available. They do this mainly to attract new customers, but having invented a new kind of account with a high interest rate, they often neglect to tell their existing customers about it, leaving them in their old accounts which pay less. It is an understandable oversight, but it does mean that you must be constantly vigilant in order to obtain the best rate of interest for your bank savings.

A new kind of account is now becoming common that merits some attention from the careful investor. This combines a current account with a house mortgage loan. The idea is that the account represents the total of all money borrowed, money saved, and money normally held in a current account. Interest is charged daily on the net debt. If you pay your salary into the account at the beginning of the month, your total debt will be reduced and you will pay less interest for a short time.

If you also save from your monthly income, leaving the savings in this kind of account will reduce the interest payment on your total loan. Effectively, you will be getting the same interest on your savings as you are paying on your mortgage. Money saved in this way can be subsequently taken out of the account so long as the total debt does not exceed the amount originally agreed for the mortgage contract.

This is a good way of keeping all your debts in one account and therefore under tight control. It is also a very effective way of combining short-term money management with long-term mortgage debt. For the private investor, there is the additional bonus that money held as cash between investments can be used to reduce mortgage interest payments, effectively it receives interest at the mortgage rate.

Government Bonds.

The Bank of England was originally a private bank founded in 1694 to supply the government with loans at a low rate of interest. These bonds were said to be 'as good as gold', and so became known as 'Gilt-edged', or simply 'gilts'. A bond is simply an IOU given in exchange for a loan. It promises to repay the debt on a stated future date and to pay interest at a fixed rate at specified intervals. The fact that the British Government has made this promise gives gilts a special place as the most secure of investments. In the three hundred years during which such bonds have been issued, the interest has been paid promptly, and every one has been repaid on time.

The first bonds were issued to pay for foreign wars. They were a great success. More and more were issued as earlier ones became due for payment, and the government need for cash increased. At the time, it seemed as if the government was getting itself into a terrible debt situation. However, as the loans mounted and the interest payments increased, so did economic activity. The result was that the government found itself with more tax revenues from which to pay the interest on the bonds.

This benign cycle of money supply expansion and increased tax revenue continued for two hundred years, from the early 1700s to 1914. In retrospect, is seems clear that the high economic growth and low inflation during these two hundred years was partly due to the expansion of government debt, which facilitated increased money supply. However, throughout this period, there were persistent calls for debt reduction and decreases in government expenditure, as there still are today.

One of the great benefits of national debt for British citizens, was that it provided a very secure way of saving for many people of middle income. For the first time in our history, it was no longer necessary to hoard gold and silver coins. A portfolio of gilts could provide a steady income in old age for the prudent saver with perfect safety. In effect, it meant that gold and silver coins, which would have been hoarded away, went to the government as payment for bonds. These receipts were promptly spent and the money was returned to the economic system. The period of economic stability that Britain enjoyed in its days of empire was partly due to this way of 'recycling' the people's savings via government spending.

The Gilts Market

Government bonds, gilts, are traditionally issued in multiples of £100, that is, the smallest number of bonds you can buy is one, and its value when repaid is £100. The period of the loan varies from about three years to thirty, but since bonds have been issued in almost every year, there are always bonds available with expiry dates from one to thirty years. Bonds carry a fixed interest payment, usually made once, twice or even four times a year.

When a bond reaches 'maturity', that is, the period of the loan expires, it is repaid at 'par'; meaning the holder receives £100 for each bond. This is called 'redeeming' the bonds, and the £100 is known as its 'redemption' value. There is an active market in bonds which have been issued in previous years, so you don't have to wait until the government or a company are making an issue. You can buy them 'second hand' on the gilts market, and what is more, you can sometimes buy them below their redemption value.

To understand why anyone should sell a £100 bond for less than £100, we need to look at the reasons why people buy bonds in the first place. Assume that the bond we are interested in was issued when bank interest rates were 10%. The savers who bought the bonds on issue might have expected interest rates to fall, so that buying these bonds would have been a good way of locking into a 10% interest rate.

However, let us assume that instead of falling, bank interest rates actually rose, say to 20%. The bond holders would have obtained more interest by keeping their money in the bank. So they would tend to sell these bonds and put their money back in the bank. But in order to sell their bonds they would have to accept a lower price than the nominal £100, since no one else would now accept 10% on a bond when they could get 20% in the bank. The bond price would therefore fall, and be available to other investors for less than £100.

The price at which a bond sells in the second hand market depends on how long the bond has to run to maturity and its nominal interest rate. If a bond is due to mature in a few months' time, its value will be very close to the £100 redemption value. If the bond had thirty years to run, its price will be determined mainly by its nominal interest rate and that of competitive bank lending rates. In the example given above, one 10% bond would pay £10 per year. If it had a long time to run it would be valued in comparison with the bank rate of 20%. So, at a price of £50, it would yield exactly 20% and its price would be about this value.

Calculating the total return on a bond is a simple matter. For example, a bond with ten years to run to maturity, with an interest rate of 5%, selling at £90, will return 10 x 100 x 0.05 = £50 in interest, and £10 in capital gain when the bond is redeemed for £100. Thus, the total return is £50+£10 = £60 on an investment of £90, which is about 66.7% over ten years, an average of 6.67%. However, this does not take into account the fact that you must wait until redemption to receive the £10 capital gain.

To arrive at a figure for effective compound interest it is necessary to separate the annual interest from the capital gain. The annual interest is £5 on £90, which is a rate of 5.55%. This is known as the running yield. After ten years, the bond will be redeemed at £100, which on £90 investment, is a gain factor of 1.111 over ten years. This is equivalent to compound annual interest of 1.06%. Putting this together with the running yield gives a total annual compound rate of 6.61%. This is known as the redemption yield - the yield if you hold the bond until redemption.

Fortunately, you do not have to do this calculation for government bonds. The running and the redemption yields are quoted daily in the financial press, together with the price at which the bonds are selling in the market.

Company and Municipal Bonds

Other large organisations often issue bonds in order to raise ready cash for investment or to pay a debt. Municipal bonds are those issued by Town and City Councils, and since they are more or less backed by the government they are seen as only slightly more risky than gilts. Thus the interest that they pay is only just above that of gilts, and essentially they work in the same way.

On the other hand, company bonds are less secure, because if the company goes bankrupt their bonds may become worthless. However, when a company does go bust, the bond holders are second in the line of creditors after the banks. They are paid ahead of shareholders out of any cash remaining after the company has paid its bank debts. The interest rate on company bonds depends on the relative risk that the company will fail. For example, large public utility companies such as electricity plc's are seen as more secure than consumer product companies selling, for example, ice-lollipops, simply because they are less dispensable to the economy. Better security means lower interest rates, and in the bond market, yield and risk are very closely aligned.

When a company issues bonds, it sometimes gives them less priority than other bonds it has in issue. This means that the new bond holders will not get equal treatment should the company fail. The existing bond holders will be paid first. Only if there are funds left, will the new bond holders be paid off. The reason for this is that the original bond holders insist that their interest in the company is not 'diluted' by the issue of new bonds. The new bond issue will therefore be stated to be subordinated to the existing one. This explains why bonds from the same company often have different prices and different interest rates,

One of the inventions of the financial services industry in recent years is the 'junk' bond. This is a bond which has been issued with a very low priority. Consequently its quality is seen as 'junk' and the interest paid on such bonds is exceptionally high. Such bonds can be very profitable to own when the company is doing well, but their price can fall dramatically at the first sign of bad news.

Another innovation is the 'permanent interest bearing bond' (PIB). These are simply bonds issued with no maturity date. They are a popular with building societies, and since they will never be repaid, their return is easy to calculate. Their virtue is that they pay high interest and can be traded easily on the appropriate market.

However, like any other bond, even a hint that the dividend will not be paid and their price drops rapidly.

Preference Shares in Public Companies

Preference shares are not really shares at all - they are more like bonds with a low priority. They pay fixed interest, which is called a dividend, and are repaid at par when they expire. Many companies issue preference shares as a way of raising cash quickly and cheaply. The shares are similar to junk bonds in that they rank below other fixed interest debt, but above ordinary shares. Like a bond, the preference share has a fixed dividend. However, the company is only obliged to pay it if there are sufficient profits to do so. Thus, at the first hint of trouble, the preference shares fall in price. One way of making preference shares more attractive is to issue them as 'cumulative'. That is, if a dividend is missed, then it must be paid as soon as the company is able to do so.

An additional sweetener for preference shares is when they are issued with the right to convert them to ordinary shares at some fixed price. This gives them a flavour of ordinary shares, yet guarantees the dividend. If the company grows quickly, and the price of ordinary shares rises accordingly, then the preference shares can rise above their issue price.

For example, a preference share might be issued at 100p with a dividend of 5% and a right to convert to ordinary shares on payment of a further 50p. Thus, if the ordinary shares stand at 80p it is clearly not worthwhile for the holder of the convertible preference shares to convert at a cost of an extra 50p per share. However, if the company grows, and after a few years the ordinary shares stand at 160p, then it will pay the preference shareholder to convert their preference shares to ordinary shares.

He has already paid 100p for the preference share and the additional 50p to convert makes his total outlay per ordinary share equal to 150p, as against the market price of 160p. This increase in price of the ordinary shares is reflected in the price of the preference shares. In the above example, the preference shares would trade at about 110p. Like all financial instruments, preference shares, with and without conversion rights have their place in a portfolio. They can provide good income at the same time as having potential for capital gain.

Shares in Public Companies

The concept of owning a share in a company is quite complicated. Being a shareholder involves some responsibilities and some privileges. As a shareholder in a private company you can become liable for the company's debts. The owners of a private business are responsible for its operations and may be liable for the debts of the business should it fail. This is quite dangerous unless you are an active partner and can keep an eye on how the company is being run. Fortunately, holding shares in a Public Limited Company has few responsibilities even though the shareholder has the privilege of being able to share in the company's profits. The shares which are bought and sold on the stock exchange are shares in Public Companies, or more specifically, Public Limited Companies - plc's.

The word 'Limited' is very important since it refers to the fact that the shareholders of these companies have limited liability for any losses that the company might incur. This makes it sensible for ordinary investors to risk their savings by buying shares in such companies. Without this guarantee of limited liability, buying a share would leave the investor liable for the debts of the company. As the law stands, a share owner in a public limited company does not incur liability for the company's debts if the company goes bankrupt. There is, of course, the loss of value of the shares themselves, which can be quite considerable, but no one will come and sell your house to recover the company's debts.

The main responsibility of a shareholder in a public limited company is to elect suitable managers for the company, and to ensure that they behave properly in fulfilling their duties in running the company. Unfortunately, this bit of company democracy is not taken very seriously by most small shareholders. Understandably, they are mainly interested in the profit and loss situation. Thus, it is left to the larger shareholders to supervise the activities of the board of directors. The large shareholders are almost always the 'Institutions' that is, Pension Funds, Insurance Companies, Unit Trusts, and Investment Trusts.

The privilege of owning shares in a company is that the shareholders share in the profits of the company in exact proportion to their holdings. Payment of profits is known as paying a dividend, and these payments are made one or more times a year. The exact amount of the dividend is declared as an amount per share, and is paid within a certain period after the declaration date. There is usually a small drop in the price of shares on the day that the dividend is declared, because the shares are then sold and bought 'ex-dividend'. This means that the buyer loses the right to the dividend just declared. This is retained by the seller, even though he will receive it after he has sold the shares. The dividend declaration day is thus an important date for buyers and sellers of shares since it affects the share price and the important matter of who gets the dividend.

Shareholders' Meetings

It is a requirement of the Company's Act that annual accounts for the company must be prepared in a specified way and presented to shareholders at an annual general meeting. At this meeting, the directors of the company are obliged to answer questions from shareholders, and present themselves for election to their directorships.

The board of directors usually consists of members of the company's management together with several 'non-executive' members. In this context, 'non-executive' means that the person is not an active manager of that particular company. Usually, the Chairman of the board of directors is a non-executive member, and the chief executive is the managing director.

Occasionally, a company will need to consult its shareholders in order to give them special information or ask their permission to embark on some new enterprise. Then an extraordinary general meeting will be called. The call for such a meeting can also come from shareholders themselves if a sufficient number (in terms of shares) decide that a meeting is necessary. For example, the management may decide that a take-over of another company is advisable, and will call a meeting to present their proposals to the shareholders. Or perhaps the shareholders, hearing a rumour that the company is in financial difficulties, will call a meeting in order for the management to clarify the situation.

Shareholder democracy works quite well, usually, with one proviso, the largest shareholders are usually investment institutions and since they are run by managers, their interests sometimes conflict with those of smaller shareholders. This is particularly obvious in the case of management remuneration, where the managers of investment institutions have an interest in promoting the idea that managers need to be paid very high salaries. Otherwise, shareholder democracy is efficient in ensuring that incompetent managers are soon replaced, and dishonest ones quickly detected and dismissed.

Options

In many ways, buying and selling shares is like gambling. However, unlike gambling, everyone can win if share prices generally rise, and everybody loses if they universally fall. The gain or loss is the difference between the price of the shares on buying and selling. For long term investors, short term rises and falls in the markets are of no concern because in the long term the price of shares in good companies always rises.

However, for those who like to buy and sell short term, hoping for a quick gain, the options market has significant advantages over buying and selling in the 'cash' market. Options on shares are a way to gamble on price changes, either up or down, without having to commit capital to actually buy shares. Options are available on the shares of major public companies, foreign currencies, and the indices of major markets.

An option is simply a contract which gives the buyer the right to buy or sell a particular financial instrument, on or before a future date, at a given price. Option terminology is difficult, and to avoid confusion, we will refer to 'purchasing' options, and use the buy/sell words to describe the type of option. Unlike bets in gambling, options are traded in a market and for each purchaser of an option, there is a seller, or 'writer' as the jargon has it.

The writer of an option is the person who undertakes to buy or sell the shares at the future date if you chose to 'exercise' your option. If the share price goes against you, there is no obligation for you to buy or sell, you simply lose the money you paid to purchase the option. This money goes to the writer who took the original risk. The purchase price of an option is related to the possible change which may take place in the underlying share price over the period of the option and not to the absolute price of the shares.

In understanding options, confusion can arise because a person may purchase an option either to buy or sell shares. A person may also write an option to buy and sell shares. Thus there are four possible positions to be in and these are set out below.

	(Put Option)	**(Call Option)**
Purchaser's option	To Sell	To Buy
Writer's promise	To Buy	To Sell

The option writer promises to sell shares to the purchaser of a buy option, and he promises to buy shares from the purchaser of a sell option. As we shall see, writing options is a dangerous game best left to the professionals. So, we can simplify matters by assuming that we are only interested in purchasing options.

To be clear, let's think of an option contract as a piece of paper, so that we purchase a contract that someone else has written. The contract itself is a promise by the writer to do one of two things depending on the type of option. The writer promises to either allow us to buy shares from him at a given price, or to sell shares to him at a given price, on or before a specified date.

The price at which the shares may be bought or sold in the future is called the strike price. The actual date at which the option expires is called the expiry date and is usually up to nine months ahead. An option to sell shares at the strike price is called a 'put' option, (put shares on the market). An option to buy shares at the strike price is known as a 'call' option, (calling shares from the market). Because options are purchased in a market, the holder does not have to wait until the expiry date to take his profits. He can sell his option back to the market before it expires at the market price. An option that can be sold back at a profit is said to be 'in the money'.

For the purchaser of an option, the losses are limited to the money he pays for the option contract. However, for the writer of an option, the loss is not limited. If the shares he promises to sell at the future date go up, the writer still has to buy them from the market in order to sell them to you at the strike price. Usually, the purchaser of an option that expires profitably does not actually buy or sell the shares specified in the contract. He accepts the difference in price between the strike price and the market price.

Since it is a contract that is purchased and not actual shares, its price is considerably less than the price of the share. For example, British Telecom shares, at the time of writing, are 650p. For only 77p I can purchase a 'put' option to sell a BT share at 700p in five months' time. Clearly, if BT shares fall significantly over the next five months, then I can make a profit.

All that needs to happen is that the price falls below 623p (=700-77) by the expiry date. Lets assume it actually falls to 600p then the expiry value is

100p (700-600) which is 23p profit. This is a profit of about 30% in five months. If the price does not fall as far as 600p, and ends at or above 700p, then the option expires valueless and my loss is 100%. All that I can lose is 100% - this seems a lot. However, when we come to look at futures we will find that losses are effectively unlimited

The other type of option is a call option, and at the time of writing, for 35p, I can purchase a 'call' option to buy a BT share at 700p in five months' time. Therefore, if the BT share price rises over the next five months, then I can make a profit. All that needs to happen is that the share price rises above 735p (700 + 35) before the expiry date. Lets say that it rises to 750p, then the call option will expire with a value of 50p (750-700), a profit of 15p, which is nearly 43%. Again, if the price doesn't rise above 700p, then my loss is 100%.

In both of the examples given above, the value of the option will vary from day-to-day as the actual price of BT shares goes up and down. If the share price rises steeply, the price of the call options will rise also. If I have a call option, I may decide to take the profit and sell the options back to the market rather than risk the price falling again before the expiry date.

Since the price of an option depends on the difference between the share price and the strike price, the price movements of options are a magnified version of the corresponding share price. This is what makes options attractive. They are said to be 'geared' or 'leveraged' - terms which refer to this price magnification effect.

Options are risky, and should be approached with caution. There are no long term investments in options, the longest dated are usually about one year. Since there is no actual buying or selling of shares, the holder of an option has no right to dividends. The gain, if any, depends purely on guessing the direction of price changes, and these changes have to be significant to make the options profitable.

The money that purchasers of options gain or lose is lost or gained by the options writers. It is what is known as a 'zero-sum' game. In addition, the brokers take their commission, so there is a net loss of money in the market. Since there are professionals in the market who make a steady living out of it, someone must be consistently losing.

Market professionals use options and shares as a way of making 'one way' bets on the market. They buy the shares and write call options, if the shares rise then they win on the shares, if they fall they win on the options. The other way round is to sell shares and write put options, if the shares fall they win on the shares, if they rise they win on the options. However, it is a very risky business and calculating the actual value of an option is very difficult.

Futures

Futures are easier than options to understand, but very much more dangerous. A futures contract is an agreement to buy or sell something at a future date, just like an option, except that the agreement is binding on both parties. When the expiry date arrives, you have to fulfil the contract whatever the price may be. Like options, futures contracts are traded on a market so that there is no need to wait until the expiry date before taking gains or losses.

The futures expiry dates are usually at three monthly intervals. So the futures contracts are to buy and sell the market items on the last day of March, June, September, and December. Each of these contract dates is available simultaneously on a rolling basis, and you can usually buy or sell up to two years ahead of the expiry date.

The contract is an equal obligation on both parties to buy and sell at the agreed price on the fixed future date. Thus, there are only two possible positions. Each participant in the market is either a buyer or a seller. In the market jargon, you either go 'long' or 'short'. Once you have entered the market as either a buyer or a seller, you are said to have an 'open position'. Eventually, you will have to 'close' this position or fulfil the contract on the day the contract expires.

Fulfilling the contract at the expiry date may be quite a serious matter. For example, if you have a contract to buy several tons of aluminium at a given price at the future date, it would be unwise to allow your position to remain open at the expiry date. If you did, then not only would you have to pay for the metal, but also take delivery of it. Of course, if you are involved in a business which uses aluminium, then you could buy your stocks of the metal in this way. However, for the ordinary trader, it is imperative to close your position before the expiry date. If you forget to do so, your broker will remind you in the strongest possible terms.

To close an open position, all you have to do is buy if you are short, and to sell if you are long. Closing your position will precipitate either a profit or a loss, depending on how the futures price has changed since you opened your position. Trading futures is effectively the same as buying and selling the items themselves. The way to make profits is to buy at a low price and sell at a higher price, or sell at a high price and buy back at a lower price.

If you are long, then the worst thing that can happen is that the price falls to zero. Since you have effectively bought at a fixed price, to close your position you will have to sell at zero price. In this case you will incur a limited loss which is equal to the price at which bought. This may be bad enough, but if you go short, an even worst thing can happen. You have effectively sold at a fixed price, and to close your position you must buy back at the market price. Since there is no limit to the rise in price that may occur, your losses are, likewise, unlimited. This is why futures trading is so dangerous.

The cost of a futures contract is small compared to the value of the item in the contract. For exchange rate futures (FOREX), the basic contract is for

$100,000 of currency, and a contract to control that amount can be purchased for about $10. Professionals who purchase large numbers of contracts do so at much less than $10 per contract. This charge has nothing to do with the value of the market item. It is simply a commission to cover the overheads of the futures market. Since the cost of the contract is not related to the potential price change of the item as it is in options, the concept of gearing or leverage does not apply in the same way.

Before you can trade futures, you have to deposit a sum of money with the futures broker known as a 'margin'. This amount is related to possible loses you will incur, which depends on the item being traded and the number of contracts you wish to trade. The money tied up as a margin can be regarded as capital investment, and the potential profits (or losses) can be regarded as a return on the capital invested.

For example, in the FOREX market, the margin requirement for a day trader is about $2000 for one contract which controls $100,000 of currency. A day trader buys and sells futures contracts during a single daily market session, and ends that day with no open positions. This means that the broker has calculated the maximum likely loss for a day trader to be $2,000. This will occur if the market moves against his position by about 2%, which is an indication of the average volatility of prices in this particular market. If you want to keep positions open for longer periods, say a week or a month, then the margin requirement will be higher because your potential losses are greater.

Since margin is related to possible losses, it is also, by the same calculation, related to possible gains. If you trade badly, you may lose all your margin. Likewise, if you trade successfully you could make a profit equal to your margin, that is 100% in a single day. This is what makes futures trading so exciting.

Different futures markets have different margin requirements which depend on the price volatility of the underlying item. Since this also determines the potential profits, the percentage profit available remains more or less constant across markets, that is, about 100% over the trading period you have selected. However, this is only potential profit. It is important to remember that it is also potential loss.

On average, without a way of predicting price changes, you would expect to lose as often as you won. So that, after paying brokers charges, you will be trading at a loss. The only way to trade profitably is to have some accurate method of predicting price changes. The prediction method need not be perfect. It only has to be right more than 50% of the time in order for you to make a profit.

The way futures trading has been described makes it seem very attractive. A profit of 100% per day seems too good to be true - and it is. It must be emphasised again that this is equally likely to be a loss. In addition, futures trading cannot be regarded as a way of investing since it takes up a lot of time, mainly just sitting and watching prices move up and down, and deciding when to buy and sell. It is more properly viewed as a business in which you risk your own capital - much like owning rented property or running a fleet of transport vehicles, except that you can be wiped out in a very short time. It is included in this review of financial instruments because it represents an extreme of risk taking, and is an excellent example of how not to invest your hard earned savings.

Futures as a kind of Insurance

Futures are available on foreign currencies, commodities, metals, oil, gas, bonds, and market indices. They are used by professionals as a kind of insurance against price movements in the underlying item. For example, if a British company has agreed to supply equipment to a customer in the USA at a fixed price in dollars, then there is a risk that before the equipment is delivered and paid for, the exchange rate may fall and leave the supplier pledged to sell at a loss.

To guard against this possibility, the company can purchase a futures contract to exchange the dollars it will earn at a fixed rate against the pound on an agreed future date. Thus, no matter what happens to the exchange rate in the mean time, the company will get its dollars changed into pounds at a known rate. Effectively, the price of the equipment has been fixed in pounds.

In the above example, the company bought assurance of a fixed exchange rate from the futures market. For the other point of view, the company disposed of its exchange rate risk to the futures market. The counter party who purchased the corresponding buy contract, effectively bought the risk, and it did so in the hope of making a profit out of the transaction. That is, the counter party had good reason to expect that the exchange rate would increase and was prepared to take the risk.

The company may also have felt that the exchange rate would rise, but doesn't want to take the risk that it would fall. So the company was prepared to forego a possible gain in order to eliminate a possible loss.

This buying and selling of risk is the essence of futures markets. Many companies do not want the risk of making a loss, and are prepared to pay the market to take the risk. The futures market in exchange rates is relatively calm compared with that in commodities and metals. Here the underlying items are traded on world markets in large volumes and are subject to the uncertainties of the weather, political decisions, and commercial events throughout the world.

For example, the price of oil on the world market is constantly moving due to production and demand changes in every country of the world. In addition, it is subject to political influence as oil producers try to operate cartels, and oil consuming countries put pressure on cartel members to break their agreements. The oil market rises and falls on rumours, and the oil futures market follows these changes more or less faithfully. Unlike options, the price of futures is not magnified. The gearing or leverage effect comes from the ability to purchase futures contracts at very low prices.

If you purchase a futures contract to buy, the counter-party in the deal agrees to sell, and vice versa, so that buy/sell futures contracts are always created in equal numbers. The total gains therefore, always equals total losses. Thus futures, like options, are a 'zero sum' game. In order for you to win, someone else has to lose. In the case of futures the losers are usually organisations who use futures contracts to guard against loss in a cash market transaction.

Chapter Three

Buying and Selling Stocks and Shares: How the markets work

Buying and Selling

If you want to buy or sell stocks and shares, all you have to do is pick up the telephone, call your stock broker, and give him your instructions. It really is as easy as that. However, before you can do such a simple thing, there are several preparations that need to be made. First, you have to open an account with a broker, and usually you will have to pay in advance for your first purchase. Secondly, you need to know exactly how to give your instructions. Thirdly, you need to know what stocks or shares to buy or sell. The art of wise investing will be described in a later chapter. This one will explain the mechanics of buying and selling and how the markets work.

Costs of Trading

Assuming you have an account with a broker and that you want to buy shares in a particular company. You need first to be sure that the company's shares are traded on the London Stock Exchange (LSE). It they are and the market is open, then your broker will be able to deal for you within minutes, if not seconds. You can either ask to buy a certain number of shares, or if you have a fixed amount of money to invest, you can ask to buy shares up to that value. Either way, you will incur two extra charges over and above the cost of the shares. The first is the broker's commission. This varies depending on the amount of money you are investing. The second is Stamp Duty of 0.5% of the value of the shares you are purchasing. This charge only applies if you are buying shares and not if you are selling. Stamp Duty is a government tax with no purpose other than to raise revenue.

Traditionally, the broker's commission was a fixed percentage of the value of the shares, both on buying and selling, usually between 1% and 5%. With the advent of electronic trading, these charges have come down and now some brokers make a fixed transaction charge, usually between £20 and £50. This is fair, since it takes just as much time to trade £100 worth of shares as it does £100,000 worth. However, some brokers still want a percentage, but they will usually be willing to reduce the percentage for large value trades.

If you are buying shares, it is wise to have the money already in an account with your broker, (where it will receive interest) because the amount is due seven days later. If it does not reach him by then, your broker will put your account into debit and you will then pay interest to him. Furthermore, if you do not pay up within a given period, the broker has the right to sell your shares to recover the debt.

There is an additional complication if you are selling shares. Once the deal has been agreed, you will have to send your share certificates, together with a sale form, to your broker within the seven day settlement period. You can save yourself a lot of hassle sending and receiving share certificates, if you allow your broker to be the 'nominee holder' of your shares. That is, he retains the certificates on your behalf, and when you sell shares the certificates are already with him. Generally, he will act as nominee holder for a small fee, or even no fee at all.

So far, we have talked about buying and selling shares. The procedures described above are the same when buying preference shares. Again, it is necessary to know which preference shares you wish to buy and how much you want to invest. The charges are exactly the same, including the government tax, provided they are traded on the LSE.

Buying and selling bonds is somewhat more complicated. Some government bonds are available for sale in post offices, and like national savings' certificates, no commission is charged. Other government bonds, and bonds issued by companies, must be purchased via your broker and commission will be charged when buying and selling.

Finding a broker

Finding a broker is not difficult, and the financial press regularly carry advertisements for all the leading brokers. Stock Brokers provide two kinds of service for their clients. The traditional kind in which the broker will give advice as well as executing your instructions. The more recent kind is one in which he offers no advice and just carries out your instructions whatever they are. The latter kind are called 'execution-only' brokers. More and more people are making their own investment decisions and since brokers charge extra if they give advice, execution-only trading is cheaper and growing in popularity.

You have a wide choice in your search for a stock broker. They range in size from small, local offices, to international firms who have large telephone dealing rooms. Most large towns and cities now have brokers who offer services over a counter, and they are happy to see you in person. They have the same electronic facilities as the big brokers and can deal just as quickly.

The larger brokers are accessible only via telephone, but these are manned continuously during trading hours and for some hours before and after trading. Some large brokers have telephone staff to take the orders, which they pass on to other staff who do the trading. This means that you do not get immediate confirmation that your trade has gone through. On a busy day you may have to wait hours before your order is executed.

Taking advantage of economies of scale in this way allows brokers to cut their costs and keep their dealing charges down. So cheaper services tend to be less direct. It is now possible to give your orders to some brokers via the internet. Again, this will lead to cheaper trading, but it will mean delays and a loss of immediacy

Once you have decided which broker to use, you can telephone him and ask for an application form to open an account. When you have completed this form and sent in any initial money to open the account, the broker will reply telling you your account number. When you want to trade, it will be necessary to quote your name and account number, but apart from that, the broker will trust that you are who you say you are. This system seems insecure, but it works very well, and makes buying and selling stocks and shares incredibly simple.

What the broker does

When you tell your broker which shares or bonds you are interested in buying or selling, he will go to the appropriate market to find out the price at which you can buy or sell. This is done electronically via computer driven trading screens, so the broker will be able to quote a price to you within seconds of your asking. If you agree to accept the price quoted, then the broker will make the trade and the deal is done. It really is as simple as that.

For shares in large public companies, the broker can trade for you via his trading screen. For shares in smaller companies, he will need to telephone a market maker to execute the trade. This takes an additional few minutes, and the broker may ask you to wait while he makes the call, or offer to call you back when the trade has gone through.

If the price that the broker quotes is not acceptable to you, and you want to buy at a lower price than that quoted, then you can place a 'buy at limit' order. That is, an order to buy when (and if) the price falls to your stated limit.

On the other hand, if you are selling shares, you can place a 'sell at limit' order, and the broker will sell your shares when (and if) the price rises to your limit. The broker will hold your order for as long as you want him to, within a reasonable time period. You may want to hold the order for a day, a week, or a month, beyond that it would be wise to review your limit.

Trading by telephone is now common practice and the whole process works well. The system is based on trust - trust by the broker that you are who you say you are, and trust by you that the broker will faithfully carry out your instructions. There is rarely any attempt at fraud, but occasionally there is a mistake.

Your broker may have misunderstood your instruction, either because you made a mistake in saying it, or because he misheard what you said. Such cases are surprisingly few, but to safeguard both you and himself, the broker takes the precaution of tape recording all the telephone orders he receives. In the event of a dispute, he can always replay the tape and listen to what was originally said.

Nominee Accounts

Share trading on the London Stock Exchange has a seven day settlement period. This means that the money for a share purchase must be paid within seven days, and the share certificates for a share sale must be sent in within seven days. So if you buy or sell shares on Tuesday, you must 'settle' by the Tuesday of the next week. Since most people need prompting, either to pay or to send in certificates, these seven days are easily taken up in receiving and sending letters. A simple postal delay can wreck the whole process.

Brokers are very much in favour of nominee accounts because it avoids all the delays that can occur with share certificates. Most brokers are willing to administer a nominee account for you entirely free of charge. The nominee account is not quite as simple as it was described above. The broker does not have a cupboard full of the share certificates belonging to his nominee clients. In fact, he has no paper shares certificates at all - the whole process is electronic.

The broker holds a large number of shares in a wide variety of companies on behalf of his clients. He is the legal owner of these shares. His accounts register shows that you have legal rights to the shares you have paid for and also the dividends. Just like an account of money, the broker holds the total of his clients' money in his own bank account. It is only on his internal accounting system that he registers your legal right to the money you have paid into your account with him.

If you have a nominee account and a money account with your broker, then buying and selling shares is very simple indeed. All the broker has to do is buy or sell the shares to your order, and make appropriate adjustments on his records of money and share ownership. There is no writing or cashing of cheques, there is no signing of share transfer certificates, no licking of stamps, no posting of letters. You can easily understand why brokers are so keen to have you open a nominee account. It saves his staff time and trouble, which translates into lower costs for him and a less expensive service for you. Once you have made the call giving your broker your buy or sell instructions, that is the end of it. You will receive a confirmation of the deal for your own records, but you do not have to do anything more.

There is one serious disadvantage with nominee accounts. Since you are not the legal owner of the shares, you do not appear on the company's register of shareholders. This means that you have no voting rights, and the company will not automatically send you a copy of its annual report. In addition, dividends are not paid to you directly but to the broker, who passes them on to you.

This lack of direct ownership may not seem serious if you have no wish to go to shareholders' meeting and vote. A greater problem arises in that the broker is now the legal owner of very large share holdings in many companies - much the same as a large investment fund. This allows the broker to use his accumulated voting powers to influence company policy. Nominee accounts undermine company democracy, the true owners do not vote on important issues. These decisions are taken by the managers of investment funds and nominee accounts, and as managers they have interests which are different from those of the true owners. An example of this is the growing controversy of the remuneration and service contracts of company managers. The interests of the true owners are vitally different to those of stock brokers and fund managers, who generally are all in favour of highly paid management on generous service contracts.

However, from an individual point of view, nominee accounts make light work of investing and are to be recommended. One can always obtain company reports by simply telephoning the company office. As for attending shareholders' meetings, they are often an exercise in frustration anyway.

The Markets

For every buyer there is a seller, and for every seller there is a buyer. This must be true whatever the method by which shares are traded. At the present time the shares in public companies are bought and sold in two ways. The first is via professional market makers who must always quote prices at which they are willing to buy and sell shares. The second is via computer order matching.

In a 'made' market, the price at which market makers are willing to buy (bid price) is always slightly lower than the price at which they are willing to sell (offer price). This difference, known as the 'spread', is their profit margin. These prices are valid only for a limited number of shares, known as the 'block' size. To buy or sell a number of shares greater than the block size, your broker has to get a special quotation from the market maker for the number you want to trade. The market maker may increase the price if you want to buy, or reduce it if you want to sell. However, the market maker must always quote a price, even though, in the event of very large trades, he may need time to calculate a price. He must also report the trades that he makes, though for some large orders he does not need to do this immediately. Not surprisingly, the stock exchange rules for market makers are largely to their advantage.

In order to be able to buy and sell shares, the market maker has a store of shares he can sell and an amount of money he can use to buy shares. As shares are bought and sold, the market maker adjusts the bid and offer prices so that neither his store of shares nor his money goes to zero. If the bid/offer prices he is quoting lead to his supply of shares falling and his money increasing, then he will adjust the bid/offer prices upwards. On the other hand, if his store of shares increases and his money decreases, he must adjust the bid/offer prices downwards. The market makers are professional traders and they are very skilful in anticipating changes in demand for a particular share, consequently prices can move very quickly when they need to do so.

The maker of a market in a particular share carries out his buying and selling transactions by telephone. Again, the system works on trust and again, tape recordings of the transactions are used to resolve disputes. However, the trades and the bid/offer prices are broadcast to brokers by a computer system, and appear on the brokers trading screens.

The second kind of market in shares is a fully electronic one, known as SETS, short for Stock Exchanges Electronic Trading System. This works by matching orders from brokers and it is done entirely via computers and Trading Screens. In this case, the prices posted on the screen are invitations to buy and sell shares at particular prices. A broker can execute buy and sell orders electronically, via his computer, simply by accepting the prices quoted on his screen.

These invitations to buy and sell shares which appear on the screen are posted there by other brokers. For example, if a broker has a buy limit order, he can post it on the SETS system, inviting other brokers to sell at the limit price. Similarly, if he has a sell limit order, he can post it on SETS and invite other brokers to buy at the limit price.

In the SETS market, the buying and selling is directly between brokers acting for their clients. No third party market maker is involved. Thus the difference between the lowest invitation to buy, and the highest invitation to sell, represents a genuine difference of buying and selling needs and is not a profit margin as in the case of made markets. However, this difference in price is still referred to as the 'spread'. This is confusing because it implies that order matching via computer is not as effective as a 'made' market.

Since no one is taking profit from each deal on the SETS system, it is clearly a more efficient mechanism for trading shares. It is also fairer, because everyone can see what prices are available and what trades have been done. It is likely that all shares quoted on the LSE will eventually be traded in this way, as they are in other major financial centres of the world. At the time of writing, only the top 100 public companies and a few others are traded on SETS. Bonds, preference shares, and shares of all other companies are traded through market makers.

The Stock Exchange

Since there is great potential for fraud in buying and selling stocks and shares, it is important that dealings be kept under strict control. In the UK, the organisation which oversees the buying and selling of shares is called the London Stock Exchange (LSE). The LSE is effectively a stock brokers' cartel. It represents their interests, though it is increasingly under pressure from the Bank of England to consider other interests. The way the LSE has resisted the introduction of the SETS trading system is a reflection of the interests of market makers in perpetuating the traditional methods of trading. We cannot blame them for wanting to hold onto their jobs which electronic trading will make redundant.

The LSE set the rules whereby companies are permitted to market their shares to investors via the Stock Exchange. Usually, the companies argue that the Exchange is too strict, while investors complain that it is not strict enough. In general, the dealings on the London market are fair and proper compared with those on some foreign exchanges.

This does not mean, however, that there is never any illegal activity. The main form of cheating, for which the LSE is perpetually vigilant, is called 'insider trading'. Insider refers to someone inside a quoted company who has knowledge of the company's affairs. It is illegal to use this information before it has been released to the public.

For example, if the chairman of a company knows his company is the object of a take-over bid, which will increase the share price, he could buy shares before this information is released to the public. The sub-sequent rise in the share price would enable him to make a quick profit. This kind of activity is expressly forbidden by the LSE - even if it is the Chairman's bother-in-law who uses the information, or anyone else who receives 'price-sensitive' information from someone inside the company.

Not surprisingly, the LSE takes a more relaxed attitude to cheating by brokers themselves. There seem to be no rules to stop brokers using price sensitive information about trading orders from their clients. For example, a fund manager may ask the broker to buy a very large number of shares in a company, so that the share price is certain to rise during the buying process. The broker can use that information to buy shares for himself before he buys them for his client. It does not seem fair that he should do so, but it is not illegal or even against the rules of the stock exchange.

It is a general problem throughout financial markets, that those who operate the markets, are frequently engaged in dealing via the same market. Thus they are effectively in competition with their own clients, and since they know their clients' intentions, they have an unfair advantage.

The London Financial Markets

The London Stock Exchange is just one of many markets that trade financial instruments in London. The LSE is the market for shares in public companies. The other major markets are the bond market, the foreign exchange markets, the commodities and metals market, and the futures market. It's unlikely that you will want to deal on any of these except the LSE, but an explanation of what they do will complete the picture of London as a world financial centre.

Investment professionals participate in several markets, obtaining from each some advantage that the others do not provide. For example, shares and options can be played against each other as described above, and foreign currencies and their futures can be combined to give advantages that each separately does not have.

In the days of Empire, London was the centre of a world trading system. Because Britain was the first country to trade on a truly global scale, it found itself not only exporting its own goods, but also importing and re-exporting those of other countries. It became the centre for markets in both manufactured goods and raw materials. In Victorian times, the great warehouses of London's dock lands stored the produce of the world.

In addition, and more importantly, in order to facilitate this global trade, London began to provide financial services, lending money for purchase, guaranteeing payments, etc. This financial system was based on a British pound fully exchangeable for gold, and for a period of time before the first world war, became the world's trading currency.

The British banks flourished, and were the main providers of finance required for world trade. Britain also provided most of the shipping to carry goods from port to port around the world, even for goods that did not come through its docks. Finally, London also provided insurance for the goods in transit. The reasons for London's pre-eminence in trade were largely that it was first in the field in providing this complete range of trading services. After 1914, this situation gradually declined. Other great cities started their own markets, and more convenient port facilities became available in other countries. However, the City of London still has its financial services industry. After the second world war, the USA became the dominant country for world trade, and the US dollar became the trading currency.

The most important institution in the City of London is the Bank of England. This began as a private bank with special privileges but is now the UK Central Bank, and as such, charged with setting interest rates and supervising banking in the UK. It is appropriate that the commercial banks have their headquarters only a short distance away in the city. These big banks lend to UK companies, UK citizens as well as other organisations around the world.

In the days before electronic communications, traders in the various markets had to deal face to face at a single location. This kind of trading is known as 'open outcry' and it is exactly that. The traders stand together in a confined area known as a 'trading pit' and shout prices and quantities at each other. From the outside, it sounds like chaos, but the traders understand each other very well, and enormous amounts of dealing can be carried out in a short time. The Stock Exchange building is where face-to-face trading took place before it was replaced in the 1980's by electronic trading. Trading in shares is now distributed with market makers in different locations throughout the city.

In the old days, the Royal Exchange was the market location for foreign exchange trading, as well as the Lloyds insurers. Now foreign exchange dealing is done by telephone and is distributed around the city in the offices of the big banks. This market also offers forward contracts in all the major currencies. Lloyd's, the insurance company, now has its own modern building.

In the times when Britain had the biggest merchant fleet in the world, arrangements for shipping were made on a market known as the International Shipping Exchange. This was housed in a building called the Baltic Ex-change, which was destroyed by a terrorist bomb in the 1990's. This market now operates in a smaller building and it still transacts international business.

As the centre of a great trading empire, the City of London developed markets in two classes of traded raw materials - Metals and Commodities. The London Metals Exchange still trades seven different metals in face-to-face dealing in addition to hedging contracts. The metals traded are copper, zinc, lead, aluminium, aluminium alloy, nickel, and tin. The gold market is run separately by the London Bullion Market Association under the supervision of the Bank of England.

The London Commodity Exchange trades a wide range of 'soft' and agricultural commodities, again in face-to-face trading, as well as futures and options contracts. The commodities are cocoa, robusta coffee, sugar, barley, wheat and potatoes. Smaller commodities such as spices and nuts are traded between agents, and tea is sold by auction. This exchange also trades futures in these products. In addition, it operates a futures market for freight called BIFFEX - the Baltic International Freight Futures Exchange.

In recent times, London has developed other markets as needs arose. The discovery of North Sea Oil led to the founding of the International Petroleum Exchange. This now trades a range of energy products, derived from oil and gas, as well as futures and options on them.

However, most important of all is the London International Financial Futures Exchange - LIFFE. This is a new innovation offering futures and options on short term interest rates and government bonds of several major industrial nations. LIFFE also offers options on the UK stock market indices and on the share prices of most companies in the FTSE100.

London is now rivalled by other financial centres throughout the world. Round the clock trading is now a major requirement so it is unlikely that any one place will ever become the unique market for financial services that London once was.

In fact, with the advent of electronic trading, the markets are becoming even more distributed and it is no longer necessary for traders to gather together in one place at a special time. New York, Tokyo, and Frankfurt all have active financial centres which rival London. Chicago is a centre for futures trading, and its market is open 23 hours a day.

When the UK joins the European Common Currency, as surely it must, the City of London will gradually fade in significance as a financial centre. The European Central Bank will be in Frankfurt, so the Bank of England will no longer be central, and the major British banks will become minor European ones. London will follow Athens, Rome, Genoa, Venice, and Bruges, down the lane of history as centres of great trading empires.

Chapter Four

Past and Present Masters

Stock market masters

It is only in this century that men have become immensely rich entirely by investing in companies that they did not control. Throughout history there have been talented businessmen running companies of various kinds - Rockerfeller in oil, Morgan in banking - who became the richest men of their times by hard work, hard bargaining, and sheer genius. Usually, they made money by investing other people's money in companies which they themselves controlled. They were active investors, in the most dynamic sense of the phrase.

To become rich by investing but not managing, simply by buying and selling stocks and shares in companies, requires a different kind of genius. It needs a special insight into the whole world of economics, finance and business not just a narrow niche. It also requires a deep knowledge of how financial markets work.

This chapter investigates the careers of some of these men. The way they made money is not the same in every case. In fact, each has his own particular approach and methodology. However, they all have the same qualities - their individuality, their independence of mind, and their absolute confidence in their own opinion.

All five of these outstanding investors achieved their success in the United States of America, and this is no coincidence. America is still growing, though not quite as fast as before. The fact that two of our five financial heroes were born elsewhere indicates that the United States is place where sheer talent can bring the highest success.

European countries and their stock markets are more conservative. They have many centuries of development behind them, and therefore there are fewer new regions and enterprises in which to invest.

In addition, private investors in Europe tend to be secretive and do not generally advertise their success. Even so, it is unlikely that any European investor has been as successful as the following list of market masters from America.

William Gann	1878 - 1955	Born in USA.
Benjamin Graham	1894 - 1976	Born in England, emigrated to USA 1896.
John Templeton	1912 -	Born in USA.
Warren Buffet	1931 -	Born in USA.
George Soros	1930 -	Born in Hungary, emigrated to USA 1956.

William Gann

William Gann traded on the USA stock market right through the first world war, the booming 1920's and the depressed 1930's, making money consistently, irrespective of whether the market was going up or down. During the Wall Street Crash of 1929, Gann made $13 million dollars by 'shorting' the market, that is, by selling shares he did not own and buying them back later at a lower price. In modern money that is about $500 million. There is no doubt that William Gann was a speculator rather then an investor, and one of genius. The controversy surrounding Gann lies in understanding exactly how he did it.

Gann wrote about his methods, and he also gave courses to would-be speculators. In spite of this, no one else has been able to trade as successfully as he did. Gann's trading record is phenomenal. In 1908 he is reputed to have turned $130 into $12,000 in 30 days. Later in 1923, he increased $973 to $30,000 in 60 days, and even in the depressed year of 1933, he made profits of 4000%.

The most famous story about Gann concerns his trading in wheat options. In 1909, at midday on the last day of trading for September wheat, the price was $1.08. Gann predicted that the price would go to $1.20. He is reported to have said 'If it does not touch $1.20 by the close of the market, it will prove that there is something wrong with my whole method of calculations.' In the last hour of trading, the price rose and closed at $1.20. This story sounds too neat to be true. If it is true, it seems likely that it was a publicity stunt organised by Gann with the objective of enhancing his reputation as a speculator.

Gann did not specialise in any one market, he played stocks, shares, options and futures with equal facility. All that he needed to operate was an accurate price history of the instrument he wished to trade. Gann was one of the first traders to construct charts. He plotted price against time on simple, one eighth of an inch graph paper, and made his investment decisions entirely on the basis of what he found there.

As far as we know, Gann did not read company reports, financial summaries or economic forecasts. His methods were based entirely on numbers. At various times he invoked biblical quotations, mystical prophesy, and magic numbers to explain his success. It is difficult to believe that he was sincere in this.

Unfortunately, Gann's charting methodology is ambiguous, even though he claimed that it was 'mathematical'. He constructed price charts, drawing on them price levels and trend lines. His idea was that certain price levels provided 'support' and 'resistance' to the price, and that these levels were related to each other by simple whole number ratios, 1 to 2, 2 to 3 etc.

Likewise, he believed that prices rose or fell on 'trend lines' which were at angles defined by whole number ratios, for example, 2 along the time axis, to 3 along the price axis, etc.

A study of price/time charts indicates that prices do sometimes appear to find support and resistance at 'Gann levels', and may follow trends at 'Gann angles'. However, they just as often do not. So it is easy, in retrospect, to find examples where prices have obeyed Gann's rules, but it is equally easy to find examples where they do something completely different. Since it seems equally likely that prices may or may not follow the rules, the rules themselves are somewhat useless.

Gann is important for two reasons. The first is that he made money from buying and selling on financial markets without any inside knowledge of the financial instruments he was trading. His methods obviously worked for him, his inability to pass on his intuition and insight is not unusual in gifted individuals.

His success over many decades indicates that there are predictable features in market price data, though it would appear that Gann's ability to detect it was intuitive rather than systematic. Certainly, his 'mathematical' rules do not work consistently enough to explain his enormous success.

Gann is also important because he pioneered the use of charts in stock market analysis and prediction, a method that is still preached and practised. He was the first successful practitioner of 'chartism', which is also known as 'technical analysis'. The fact that Gann was able to use charts to predict price changes and to make profits from trading has inspired several generations of 'chartists'. Modern technical analysts use digital computers and powerful signal processing algorithms. Yet, they still cannot achieve the success that Gann enjoyed. This confirms the conclusion that Gann's methods were largely based on a finely tuned intuition, and that his explanations were simply rationalisations of a process which he himself did not fully understand.

Benjamin Graham

Benjamin Graham was born in England in 1894 but his parents migrated to the USA when he was one year old. His father died when he was only eleven so the young Graham was no stranger to hardship. He attended college, studying classics and mathematics. When he began work, it was as a messenger in a firm of Wall Street stock brokers. However, he was soon contributing his own financial analysis reports and he was made a partner after only six years.

Graham was an intellectual with interests in mathematics, classical literature, philosophy and languages. He translated from Portuguese and wrote several books outside the field of finance. By the time he was 36 he was running his own investment partnership, which made money in the late 1920's but was wiped out in the severe bear market which followed the 1929 crash. For the second time in his life, Graham experienced financial disaster, and this was to shape his investment philosophy.

In keeping with his intellectual interests, Graham also taught classes at Columbia Business School. His interest in mathematics inclined him towards scientific methods of investment, and he studied company records and accounts assiduously.

In 1934, together with Professor Dodd, he published the results of his studies in the famous book 'Security Analysis'. This book was to become the basic text book for students of investment. In it he outlines his ideas on investing as opposed to speculating, and on what constitutes good investment. His main objective was to make money in a fail safe way.

Graham's insight into company financial operations enabled him to identify the characteristics of a company that allowed it to outperform other companies. His basic philosophy was simply to buy companies which had superior asset backing, and to buy as many such companies as possible in order to 'spread' the risk. He did not investigate its management or take into account general economic considerations. He worked entirely with the company's accounts, ignoring brokers' recommendations.

Benjamin Graham's essential idea was to calculate the basic value of a company from a detailed study of its assets. His strategy was to invest only in those companies where the 'quick' asset value per share was less than the actual share price, and to sell them when the share price caught up with the quick asset value. As Graham put it, 'buying a dollar for fifty cents could not fail to make money'.

Graham placed great emphasis on what he called 'safety of principal', that is, to make sure that the original investment was not reduced. He didn't believe in taking unnecessary risks and his strategy was for fail-safe investment. Using his rules, if the company fails, and the assets are sold off, the shareholder would at least get his money back and probably more. If the company grows then the shares increase in value.

In 1936, Graham began again, even though the economy was still in deep depression. His investment company achieved, on average, a return of 21% per annum for the next 30 years. Unlike some funds, he did not build up capital but returned profits to his shareholders as dividends. This meant that Graham's investment fund did not grow bigger than $20 million. His reasoning was that it would be impossible to find suitable investments for more than this amount.

In calculating the asset value of a target company, Graham usually considered only what he called 'quick assets' that is, cash and those assets which could be sold quickly for cash, approximately what in the UK are called 'liquid' assets. It seems unbelievable now, that in Graham's time, companies could be bought for less than their quick asset value. This is like being able to buy someone's wallet for less than the cash it contains. Yet, in the 1930s, after the Wall Street Crash of 1929, even professional investors were too nervous to pay higher prices. Since they were also unsophisticated, and many did not read company accounts, they were mainly unaware of these opportunities.

That share prices could sink so low in a crash is a feature of stock market behaviour. Markets tend to overreact to both good and bad news. Graham was the first fund manager to advise clients not to pay too much attention to share prices except when they have to buy or sell them.

Graham's dictum was - buy good shares on bad days. He likened stock market behaviour to that of a manic/depressive person, who he referred to as 'Mr Market'. One day, in a fit of depression, Mr Market will telephone you offering to sell you really good shares at unbelievably low prices. A few months later, in a mood of manic optimism, he calls again offering to buy them back at ridiculously high prices.

Benjamin Graham taught his investment techniques to several generations of students and they soon came into widespread use. Not surprisingly, the investment opportunities that were available earlier in this century have long since disappeared, at least in the western world.

In addition to safety of principal, Graham also wanted a company to have consistent, better-than-average growth. His method of predicting which companies would grow was simply to look at the pattern of past growth. If a company had grown consistently in the past, it was, he reasoned, more likely than others to grow in the future.

Benjamin Graham probably made less money than other great investors. Having learned the value of money the hard way, and having lived through the 1929 crash, he always put safety first. In addition, he was less interested in money than ideas, and he was generous in his advice. By publishing his ideas, he helped the whole investment community to make the stock market a more efficient arbiter of value. His fortune may have been modest, but his influence was great.

John Templeton

John Templeton was born in 1912 in Tennessee. He studied at Yale and, as a Rhodes Scholar, graduated from Oxford, UK. In 1937 he began work on Wall Street, which at that time, was still in the grip of the Great Depression. In 1939, aged 27, shortly after the outbreak of world war two, he borrowed $10,000, and invested it in 104 stocks selling for less than $1 per share on Wall Street. This list included 34 companies which were technically bankrupt.

His intuition was that the war would end the ten year depression, and the stock market would recover. He was proved right, within five years this portfolio had increased in value to $40,000, a factor of four times, and an annual growth of 32%.

After the war, Templeton began working for himself as an investment advisor, controlling assets that eventually grew to $300 million. At age 56, already a very rich man, Templeton turned away from the noise and clamour of Wall Street. He realised that working harder and harder in a busy city was not a good way to live. So, he sold his company, keeping only the Templeton Growth Fund, and moved to Nassau on the Bahamas. Here, he felt he could work just as well, and yet have time to develop his spiritual life.

Both on Wall Street and in the Bahamas, Templeton worked diligently to increase the value of his Growth Fund. When he eventually sold it to the Franklin Group, it had advanced by an average of over 16% per annum over a period of 45 years. To sustain this record for so long, was a tremendous achievement. John Templeton is also the founder of the Templeton Foundation, which annually awards the Templeton Prize for Progress in Religion. In 1987 he was given a British knighthood in recognition of his charitable deeds and his services to business.

Templeton learned the company analysis techniques pioneered by Benjamin Graham. In particular, he developed the idea of spreading risk by buying into many small companies. His great achievement was to apply these principles, not just in the United States of America, but on a world wide basis. He realised that what worked on Wall Street would work in other countries too. Funds were invested whereever bargains were to be had, and he has been particularly successful in Japan.

He specialised in finding bargain buys - companies which sell for less than their true worth - and holding them for an average of four years. Naturally, most of these companies are too small to be noticed by the big Wall Street analysts, and therefore he was able to buy them cheaply. Like, Graham, he was prepared to buy many such companies so that the averaging process would work in his favour. That is, the many good buys would more than make up for the few bad ones. Again, like Graham, he did not believe in having too much money in his fund, since this would restrict his flexibility.

Warren Buffet

Warren Buffet was born in 1931, and from an early age showed an interest in making money. He was still a teenager when he first began to invest in companies using money he made from his local business ventures. He attended university and had the good fortune to be a student of Benjamin Graham. After graduating he worked for Graham and learned all he could about Graham's investment strategies.

At the age of 25 Buffet set up his own investment fund - a partnership in which he was the manager. After 13 years, he dissolved the partnership, and returned his partners' capital to them. Those partners who had been with the fund for the whole 13 years received 30 times the amount of money they originally invested, an annual growth rate of 30%.

When Buffet closed down his partnership he was still under 40 years of age and worth 25 million dollars. Buffet realised that if he was to be really successful, he needed to be free to invest where and when he judged appropriate. To do this he used a company called Berkshire Hathaway, of which he was both principal shareholder and chief executive. This company owns the shares and Buffet manages the investments.

Because Berkshire Hathaway has a stock market quotation, Buffet's followers can buy its shares and share in his success. The shares have increased in value, on average by 26%, per annum over 30 years, with no losing years. This is a total growth factor of more than 500. This is an outstanding performance, the more so for being so consistent through many turns of market sentiment. Clearly, Warren Buffet has not just been lucky, he has considerable insight into good investing and we would be wise to pay heed to what he has to say.

Warren Buffet developed Graham's ideas of safety and growth, and established his own criteria for selection. His main innovation is to insist on understanding how a company makes its money. Buffet only invests in companies, or 'businesses', as he calls them, which he can understand. So he either avoids complicated businesses or goes to a lot of trouble to understand how they work. Basically, Buffet does not believe in spreading risk, his objective is to reduce it to an absolute minimum.

His advice is to buy shares only in those companies that you would feel happy owning and running yourself. His long term investment in some of America's most profitable companies shows that his insight into their business operations has been an important element of his success. His holdings in some of these companies are now so large that he is also a member of the board of directors, and he does, in fact, help to run these businesses.

Another of Warren Buffet's sayings is that a good business can survive bad managers whereas, a bad business will still go down even with good managers. He advises therefore to invest in good businesses rather than to follow successful management, though he prefers to have both in the companies he buys.

In answer to the question, what is a good business? Warren Buffet has a simple and direct answer - it should have the potential for sustained growth of earnings. It is worth emphasising that he focuses on earnings and not turnover or dividends. Earnings are a company's net income from its business; turnover is the total amount of cash that goes through the company's books. Dividends are simply the money that the company pays out to its shareholders. Earnings growth is a sure sign that a company has a good business.

George Soros

George Soros was born in Hungary in 1930. He lived there through world war two and emigrated to England in 1947. He attended the London School of Economics where he was very much influenced by the work of the philosopher, Karl Popper. In 1956, after a few years working in the British investment industry, he emigrated again, this time to the United States of America where he began work as a financial analyst.

After working for ten years writing investment reports, in 1968 he began his Quantum Fund, a hedging fund using options and futures to hedge longer term investments. The fund averaged over 30% annual growth for many years, though recently it has suffered setbacks. However, it still has the best growth record of any investment fund over several decades.

Soros refers to himself as a speculator, and jokes that a long term investment is a speculation that went wrong. His technique is to follow market movements and buy and sell as often as necessary to catch the major changes of market direction. He uses options and futures extensively, and likes to make money when the market falls as well as when it rises. His intuition for predicting market sentiment is remarkable and he is clearly a speculator of genius in the style of William Gann.

Soros has written about his techniques and has developed the theory of 'Reflexivity' to explain how he is able to predict boom and bust patterns of market behaviour. He is famous for predicting the breakdown of the European Monetary System in 1992. He used his fund's resources to bet against the British Pound being able to hold its exchange rate with the German Mark. When the Pound finally broke away from the EMS, the Soros funds made a profit of one billion dollars.

George Soros is also a major philanthropist. His Foundation for an Open Society takes its name from work by Karl Popper, written in opposition to the dictatorships of Germany and Russia during the second world war. His network of foundations operates in 31 countries throughout the world. He has also founded the Central European University and the International Science Foundation. He has given away approximately one billion dollars.

The Speculators

Our five market masters each have an individual style in the way they make money. However, they all show one common quality - single mindedness, the ability to stick with their own judgement no matter what the markets may do. These five have, over more than one hundred years, proved that market valuations are far from perfect, and that there are always opportunities for intelligent and independent men to make money, either by speculation or investment.

Of the speculators Gann and Soros, we can only marvel at their skill in riding the twists and turns of market movements. To be successful over many years needs considerable insight into market behaviour. Since the market is made up of other investors and speculators, predicting market behaviour is equivalent to guessing how people will react. This is what every speculator is trying to do, so the game is essentially to guess how others will guess before they actually make their guess.

Speculation is essentially gambling, and to be successful a speculator needs a keen intuition and a natural ability to read market sentiment. Like good poker players, they are able to bluff and use their buying power to advantage at critical moments. This is the reason why a reputation as a successful speculator can be such an advantage, and there is no doubt that both Gann and Soros have sought out publicity.

Speculators cannot trade without someone knowing what they are doing. At the very least, their broker has to know what the speculator wishes to do in order that he can carry out the trading plan. The successful speculator knows that people will try to make money by following his lead. He will, therefore, use this fact to his advantage.

Once it becomes known that a successful speculator is buying a certain company's shares, other speculators will rush in, pushing up the price. It is not difficult to take advantage of this effect. A speculator who is well known can easily publicise his opinions in order to change the market sentiment in his favour. His predictions will then become self-fulfilling, and so long as he can buy and sell in advance of the others, he will make more profit.

For this reason, we must be suspicious of anything successful speculators like Gann and Soros are willing to tell us. It is very unlikely that Gann based his investment decisions on mathematics, magic numbers, or biblical prophecies. In claiming these three sources of special insight, he was appealing to scientific, mystical and religious beliefs. The ability to influence other market participants gave Gann a way of enhancing the market price swings, and to exploit these for greater profits.

In the case of Soros, his claim that the theory of Reflexivity enables him to predict shifts in market sentiment, is again a way of attracting support for his investment decisions. Having attained status as a financial guru, Soros has not been slow to give his opinions on how world markets will move in the near future. We can never be sure that he is sincere, since by broadcasting his opinions he well knows that this will affect market sentiment and provide him with an opportunity for profit.

Neither Gann's levels and angles, nor Soros's Reflexivity, fully explain their phenomenal success. It would be nice to think that we could emulate them, but it is very unlikely. Many have tried but none have succeeded. The intuition needed for speculation is not easily learned, if at all. It is a gift, and no amount of theory can replace this essential ingredient. We will be well advised to avoid risking our savings by speculating on market sentiment.

The Investors

From the great investors, Graham, Templeton, and Buffet we have more hope of learning something useful. Their investment experience spans nearly a century, and they are in agreement that diligent study of companies and their financial performance can yield the information we need to make profitable investments. All three agree in ignoring the views of the market professionals and stock brokers. The differences in their investment techniques are due partly to their different temperaments, and partly to the way markets have changed during this century.

The bargains that Benjamin Graham found plentiful in the 1930's are no longer available, mainly because Graham himself revealed the secret of finding them in his famous book 'Security Analysis'. Having lived through the 1929 Wall Street crash, Graham put great emphasis on safety. His idea of looking was seek out companies with good asset backing. He advised buying as many suitable companies as possible in order to spread the risk, again a safety measure.

John Templeton applied Graham's technique on a world wide scale. He managed to find under-valued assets by searching amongst smaller companies and on markets outside the United States. Templeton developed the idea of risk spreading, and held shares in a wide variety of companies in many different markets. He avoided large popular corporations on the basis that their ability to grow was limited.

Warren Buffet finds his opportunities by looking more deeply than Graham or Templeton into the way companies work. He also talks to managers and is not afraid to join them in making critical decisions. He sees business management as essentially allocation of capital. Buffet likes to hold shares for as long as possible, and is reluctant to give up on a company once he has invested in it. However, he likes to buy at bargain prices and is willing to wait until the market falls to the right level.

If we eliminate the possibility that we can make money by speculating, then we are left with the methods of investment advocated by Graham, Templeton, and Buffet. The objective of this book is to try to take the best elements of all three, and to combine them in a way that is simple to apply.

As amateur investors, we do not have a lot of time to study companies or talk to their management. All the information we have is what we can find in company reports, the financial press, and from our own insights into the world of business. Since our time is limited, we will not be able to look after shares in a large number of companies. The next chapter attempts to provide a recipe for making investment decisions that fits in with the time and information we have available.

Chapter Five

Wise Investing

Assets as Savings

Asset prices rise and fall for a variety of reasons, but only three are important. The first is the cycle in asset prices, whereby asset prices rise and fall mainly because more or less money is available to buy them. The second reason is that, on a long term basis, asset prices trend upward because of inflation. Thirdly, the price of a particular asset may rise or fall because it has become more or less valuable.

As private investors we will need to be aware of the asset price cycle which is discussed in detail in chapter ten. We will be more inclined to buy assets when the prices are low and to sell when they are high. We will also note the effect that inflation is having on asset prices and not be deluded that inflationary gains are real. However, our main concern will be to identify assets that are increasing in value by their own 'internal dynamic'.

In the following discussions on portfolio management, a distinction will be made between a growth portfolio and an income portfolio. These are the two types of portfolios we will need. The first for building up capital while we are working, the second for providing income when we have retired.

It is natural, therefore, that shares in good quality companies will form the basis of our growth portfolio, and secure bonds will be the main components of our income portfolio. However, there will be exceptions to this rule, and one of them is the use of specialist investment trusts, which can be used to give either growth or income.

How much pension do we need

A working life of 40 years is about the most we would hope for, say from 20 to 60. If we have an extended education or retire early, we can expect less than this. In addition, many people do not start seriously thinking about pensions until they are in their thirties, and this cuts down the saving period to about 25 years. This is still a considerable time, and it gives us plenty of opportunity to build up capital.

In calculating how much pension we will need, we must, of course, take into account the effects of inflation on the pension we plan to receive. However, it is not just inflation that makes our savings less effective than they should be. By the time we retire the standard of living will be higher than it is now. So the pension that we will need, can best be projected by discounting average increase in earnings per year rather than just inflation.

In calculating how much income we will need on retirement, it is convenient to work with a standard amount, say £10,000 at today's values and project this into the future. The best way to do this is to assume that the current growth in average income will continue indefinitely. This figure is approximately the sum of inflation plus economic growth. Inflation targets are about 3% and economic growth averages about 2% per year. So, using a rate of income growth of 5%, in 25 years' time we will need about £34,000 for every £10,000 we would need now.

The next problem is to work out how much capital we will need in our growth portfolio to obtain an income of £34,000. If we use government bonds, at an interest rate of about 6%, we would need to have a capital sum of £567,000. Unfortunately, this would give us a fixed income and future increases in inflation would mean a slowly declining real income.

We could do without an income portfolio if we use our accumulated capital to buy an annuity. At the time of writing these are running at about 4% for an inflation free income. This would require a capital sum of £250,000 for an inflation free income of £10,000, or at the projected need of £34,000, in 25 years' time we would need £850,000. Annuities depend on age, and on the death of the holder, the capital becomes the property of the provider.

To obtain an inflation proof pension, we need to ensure that the capital value of our income portfolio is growing at the same rate of inflation. To do this we can invest some of it in growth stocks, or more securely, set aside some of the income from bonds to augment their value on redemption. A reasonable target, therefore, for an inflation proof pension, is about 5% of the capital sum.

Thus, for our income portfolio, we can aim for an inflation-free income of about 5% of our capital without taking too much risk. Using this figure, we would need £200,000 of capital for every £10,000 or inflation free income. On this basis, in 25 years' time we would need £680,000 to provide us with a standard of living equivalent to £10,000 at today's values.

Investing for Income

We must remember that, with bonds and preference shares, the capital is paid back at par. This means that a £100 bond will still be worth £100 in ten years' time. In the meantime, inflation will have eroded the real value of its dividend. So we should save some of the income we receive from bonds as preference shares to make up the loss in real value due to inflation. Assuming inflation is running at 3%, we should save 3% of our bond income and reinvest it so that the real value of our capital keeps up with inflation. This means that to achieve a target of 5% income we need bonds or preference shares that yield at least 8%.

There are companies who pay dividends on ordinary shares higher than those on bonds, but they are not suitable for our income portfolio because our capital will not be secure. Ordinary shares are the most vulnerable of investments if a company fails. The ordinary shareholders are last in the line to receive any payout when the company's assets are sold off. They only get some money back after the banks, the bond holders, and the preference shareholders have been paid in full.

The main reason for buying ordinary shares is that they have the potential for growth. However, those with the highest growth are usually the ones with the lowest dividend payments. However, there are special Investment Trusts which invest in ordinary shares of public companies, who, through their structure, offer reasonable dividends with good security. These are known as Split Capital Investment Trusts. Unfortunately, the way they work is somewhat complicated so we will defer discussion of these interesting shares until later.

Bonds we already know about, and government bonds, gilts, are the most secure of all. Nothing short of defeat in a world war will stop the British government from paying dividends on time and redeeming the bonds at par. The only problem is that the return may not be enough. We can get a slightly better interest rate from municipal bonds, and again they are very secure.

The British government issued a type of bond that pays an inflation free dividend, and this is an ideal investment, except that the interest rate is so low. They are called 'index-linked' gilts, and the capital is repaid at a level which reflects the rate of inflation. Unfortunately these bonds are in such high demand that the interest rate is only about 3%, too low to meet our target of 5%.

A much better return can be had from company bonds, but now we are beginning to take significant risks because it is possible that the company may fail. However, when a large company fails, we get plenty of warning. The ordinary shareholders are alert to any signs of danger, and since bond holders get paid before the ordinary shareholders, the latter will signal trouble long before it is significant to us. To keep the risks reasonable, we should only look at short dated bonds that have a high order of priority in the event of failure.

Preference shares are almost as good as company bonds. They are fixed interest and rank after bonds in the payout in cases of failure. In addition, they have some possibilities for growth if they are also convertible shares, but this is a bonus, not a requirement. In evaluating the soundness of a company and its preference shares, we can use the technique described above for judging the quality of its business.

Split Capital Investment Trusts

For those who do not want the trouble of selecting bonds and preference shares for their income portfolio, the ideal investment is in a Split Capital Investment Trust. Unfortunately, the dividend from a conventional investment trust is simply an average of the dividends of the shares it holds. Given that the trust holds good quality shares, its dividend will not be enough for an income portfolio.

However, there are special investment trusts which are able to pay higher dividends by splitting their return into growth and income components. These are the Split Capital Investment Trusts.

An Investment Trust is a company whose sole objective is to own shares of other companies. Thus, the shareholders of the trust are like members of a pooled investment club, except that the investment decisions are made by the trust's management. The shares of investment trusts are traded on the stock market and their price varies according to supply and demand in the usual way. The asset value of an investment trust is simply the value of the shares it holds, and since this is also its liquidation value, the shares have very good asset backing.

Because the trust invests over a wide spread of shares, its share price will follow the average price of shares on the market rather than those of any individual company. This reduces the risk by spreading it. Like a conventional investment trust, the split capital version makes its shares available on the market, and their value is the average value of the shares it holds. Thus the income of the trust is an average of the income of its shareholding, and its growth is likewise an average of the growth of its shareholding. By splitting its own shares into two classes, income shares and capital shares, a Split Capital Trust is able to provide for two kinds of shareholders - those who need income and those who need capital growth.

The trust might, for example, split its capital in two equal parts, so that its income shareholders will receive all the income and no capital growth, and its capital shareholders get all the capital growth and no income. The income shareholders effectively get twice the dividends they could expect if they held the trust's shares directly. The penalty is that they do not get any capital growth, and their shares are repaid at par when the trust is wound up. On the other hand, if the trust's shares fall, the income shares will still be repaid at par so long as there is sufficient capital to do so. This gives them excellent safety qualities, and these investments are very well suited to an income portfolio.

Again, the capital will be repaid at par, so we have to set aside 3% per year in order to maintain the real value of our capital.

How much do we need to save and invest?

The section above showed how we can calculate the income we will need at retirement and how we can obtain it through an income portfolio. This next section looks at the problem of how to accumulate the necessary capital so that, on retirement, we have enough to give us the lifestyle we have planned for.

Again, we shall work on the basis of a £10,000 income at today's values and we shall assume that our income portfolio will bring in a steady, 5% inflation-free income. Since the capital requirement is known, what we will discuss here is the saving and investment strategy we need to obtain this capital sum. The standard way of building up capital is to save a certain amount from our earnings each month and use it to build up our growth portfolio. Meanwhile, the investments already in the portfolio will be growing at a steady rate. The two numbers we need to estimate, are the amount we shall need to save each year and the growth rate of the portfolio.

There is a difficulty in that we cannot know in advance how much we will be able to save each year. Usually, our savings rate goes up because our salaries are increasing naturally, due to the average increase in earnings, and also because as we grow older our earning power increases. The figure we have used for average earnings growth is 5%, and this takes into account inflation and economic growth. If we decide to increase our savings by a factor of 10% each year, then this ought not to be too difficult to achieve.

Given this assumption on savings rate, we can now calculate the rate at which our portfolio needs to grow at in order for us to achieve our capital target. Taking the 25 year saving period we used before, let us assume that we begin saving at £1,000 per year, and increase this at 10% per year for the full 25 year period. Our saving will therefore increase from £1,000 to about £11,000 per year in the 25th year. The total money saved is about £98,000.

As each year passes, the capital sum increases, partly by additional saving, but mainly by portfolio growth. In calculating what growth factor we need to achieve our objective of £680,000, we must take into account the additional saving. Assuming that this is added at the end of each year, the required growth rate is 17.7%.

This would be difficult to achieve consistently, for 20 years but not impossible. We wouldn't need to be Warren Buffet to be sure of doing it. We can make it easier for ourselves in two ways: first by saving over a longer time period, and second by saving more of our income. For example, if we start our savings at £1,100 a year, we only need a growth rate of 17.0%. Alternately, we could save over 30 years and then we would need a growth rate of only 13.7%.

The table below shows the target capital required on the basis of 5% income growth and an income equivalent to £10,000 at today's values. The table also shows the growth rate required for ten different levels of annual saving. The figures show that saving more for longer has a dramatic effect on the growth rate required. Over 20 years, saving at £1,000 per year needs a Warren Buffet growth performance. Over 40 years, saving £1,500 needs only 5.9%, obtainable from an investment in government bonds.

	20 years	25 years	30 years	35 years	40 years
Target Capital	**£530k**	**£677k**	**£864k**	**£1103k**	**$1408k**
Savings		**Percentage Growth Rate**			
£1000	24.2	17.7	13.7	10.8	8.8
£1100	23.3	17.0	13.0	10.2	8.0
£1200	22.5	16.3	12.4	9.6	7.4
£1300	21.7	15.7	11.8	9.1	6.9
£1400	21.0	15.1	11.3	8.6	6.4
£1500	20.3	14.5	10.8	8.1	5.9
£1600	19.7	14.0	10.3	7.6	5.4
£1700	19.1	13.5	9.9	7.2	5.1
£1800	18.5	12.5	9.4	6.7	5.1
£1900	18.0	12.5	9.0	6.3	5.1

Table of Growth Rate required to achieve
target capital at various levels of saving.

This table can also be used in reverse. If we know what growth rate we can achieve then we can read off the amount of saving we will need to hit the target capital. For example, if we felt confident of achieving a growth rate of 15% over a period of 25 years, then we can see that we need to begin saving about £1400 a year. Note that the saving required are assumed to increase at 10% a year throughout the investment period.

Some statistical considerations

The objective of investing in stocks and shares is to gain a 'return' on our savings over and above that which we could obtain by keeping our money in a bank deposit account. Return on an investment is simply the profit it makes over a specified period of time and it consists of two parts. The first part is the cash income. This is the dividend in the case of shares, and interest payment in the case of bonds. The second part of return is the increase in the market price of the instrument over the period which you hold it, this is known as the capital gain.

The secret of wise investing is to buy those stocks and shares that have a better return, over the lifetime of the investment, than most of the others. We can only say 'most of the others' because it is certain that we will miss many profitable investment opportunities simply because they seem too risky. In fact, the risk that we perceive may be real. Statistically, out of 100 shares with a 10% chance of success, on average ten will actually succeed. However, no sensible investor would want to buy shares with only a 10% chance of success.

It is inevitable, therefore, that of the many investment opportunities that we reject as being too risky, a few will do better than the ones we accept. Its annoying, but no one, not even professional analysts, can be right all the time. Many professional investment managers are happy to achieve average performance. Remember, in investing, to be average is still to be successful, and to be better than average is to be very successful.

As well as realising that we will miss out on good investments, we need also to accept the possibility of failure. In a lifetime of investing, we will inevitably buy shares in a company which will not perform as well as we expected. In the next chapter we discuss how to recognise this unwelcome fact and what to do about it. Here we will look at the statistics of investment which are mainly in our favour, but may occasionally act against us.

Assume that we are only prepared to invest when there is, say, a 95% chance of success. This sounds like a very conservative policy, but it really means that we are accepting a failure rate of 5%. This implies that one investment in 20 will go wrong. However, this will only be true if we have enough investments to make the averages work in our favour.

If we invested in ten companies, each with a 95% chance of success, then there would be a 50% chance that all ten will perform perfectly, And a 50% chance that one out of the ten will fail. This is a situation we wish to avoid. To be surer of getting the average 5% failure rate we would need to invest in a very large number of companies. This is known as 'spreading the risk'. The higher the risk of failure the more it is necessary to spread the risk.

On the other hand, high risk means high returns, so there is an advantage in taking risks if we can spread the investment over many companies in order to average out the failure rate. However, there are good reasons for limiting the number of companies whose shares we will buy. The main one being that it is difficult to keep track of more than about seven holdings at any one time, unless we establish a professional routine. In addition, we will not find many companies which pass the strict criteria we shall impose.

Ideally, we should aim to hold, at any one time, between 5 and 10 companies in our portfolio. Over the lifetime of the portfolio, we will buy and sell many times. Assuming an average holding period of about 5 years, and a portfolio life of 25 years, the number of different companies which will pass through the portfolio is between 25 and 50. This is enough to give us assurance that the statistics will work in our favour. Using these guidelines, we should expect to have about two or three failures over the lifetime of our investments.

Investing for Growth

There are many theories, suggestions, and helpful hints in the writings of Warren Buffet, Benjamin Graham and others on how to evaluate investment opportunities. Much of this is too complex for the private investor, but fortunately, the main ideas are quite clear and can be formulated into a routine we can use to analyse a 'target' company.

Graham, Templeton and Buffet all agree that there are three aspects of a company on which a potential investor must focus. They are its asset value, its record of earnings growth, and the quality of its business. After discussing each of these three factors in turn, we will discuss a simple procedure for analysing a target company.

However, first it is necessary to address a simpler issue - which companies are suitable 'targets' for analysis. This is a very pertinent question since there are several thousand companies whose shares are on the market, and it is clearly impossible to examine them all. Unfortunately, there is no simple answer, private investors get their inspiration in a variety of ways.

Perhaps a press report about a company may bring it to our attention. This is likely if the company is in the news because it is growing at a promising rate, or because its assets are undervalued. Many investors get ideas from observing the businesses they deal with in their daily lives. For example, anyone who has bought a foreign holiday in the past few years will have noticed the market dominance of just a few companies. Quasi-monopolistic situations of this kind often allow prices and earnings to be driven up steadily.

The best advice is to watch and wait. It is important to keep reading the financial press, observing how prices of goods and services change, and looking hard at any company if its growth is above average. However, once a company has been identified as a potential investment opportunity, it must be analysed according to the three criteria given above. The result in each category must be positive before it can be declared a possible buy. Even then, it is only a 'possible' buy because, although the company may be worth owning, it will not always be possible to buy the shares at a favourable price. If this is the case, then the analysis can be put aside and taken up again if the share price falls. A wise investor always has a list of worthwhile companies, whose shares he will buy when the price is right.

The Value of a Company

Value, like beauty, is in the eye of the beholder. A company is worth only what someone is willing to pay for it. In buying shares in a company, we are making the decision that its value to us is at least equal to the price we are paying. Of course, we are only buying a very small part of the company, but the principle is the same. One of Warren Buffet's sayings is - never buy shares in a company which you would not feel comfortable owning and running yourself.

When we buy a company's shares, our valuation is based on the idea that the company's value will grow, so that when we come to sell the shares, they will be worth more than we paid for them. We are looking for capital growth. Since we are buying shares as an investment, our valuation may be called the company's 'investment value'. We will buy the share only if our investment valuation is greater than the stock market valuation.

Other people will value the company in a different way for different purposes. For example, if the company fails, then its assets will have to be sold off, or 'liquidated'. The organisation which performs this service will value the company as simply the sum of the value of its parts. On the other hand, to a company which is being taken over, the buyer values it as a going concern, and the company will be worth very much more.

When a company takes over another company, it is usually because there are good commercial reasons for believing that the two companies will be more profitable together than separately. This could be because of economies of scale, or because the two companies complement each other in the markets they serve. However, the main fact is that the take-over company will value the 'target' company at more than its usual stock market valuation.

Finally, we have the company's valuation of itself, which is recorded in the company balance sheet as 'net asset value'. This takes into account the basic value of the company's saleable assets, and also 'intangible assets' which is essentially the value of the company's management, staff, and brand image.

To summarise, five valuations that are of interest to us are:

- Take-over value
- Investment value
- Market value
- Net asset value
- Liquidation value

They are shown in order of highest to lowest, and if we are to invest in a company, then its investment value will need to be higher than its market valuation. We will discuss how to calculate investment value later, but here we need to look in some detail at ways of estimating the other valuations.

The market value of a company is simply the share price times the number of shares in issue. This is also known as market capitalisation. The take-over value is the most difficult to guess, it depends on so many unknowable factors that it is best to simply assume that it will be much more than market value.

The 'net asset value' of a company is recorded in the company's balance sheet. This is its 'book' value, which is calculated on the assumption that the company is a 'going concern'. It is usually optimistic, and its main use is that we can use it to estimate liquidation value.

To establish Benjamin Graham's 'margin of safety' we need to know the 'liquidation value' of a company's assets. That is, the value of the company if it had to cease trading and its assets were liquidated. The situation is like that of owning an old car. If the vehicle goes, then it can be sold as a going vehicle. If it doesn't go then it can always be broken up and sold as spare parts.

Once we know the liquidation value of a company we can divide it by the number of shares to obtain the liquidation asset value per share. This figure will be somewhat smaller than the share price. If it is equal to the share price then we have a fail safe situation. That is, if the company does fail and its assets are sold off, then we ought, at least, to get our money back. This is a very good situation to be in if an investment fails, but it does not automatically mean that we should buy the shares of such a company. The low share price may reflect the fact that the company is about to go bust. If this is so, the sell-off of its assets may take several months if not years and though we may eventually recover our investment we have lost the opportunity to invest in other companies.

In the present age of high asset prices, we should not be too alarmed to find that the share price is several times the liquidation asset value per share. It is difficult to be precise because different kinds of companies have different kinds of assets and different ways of making money from them.

Capital intensive companies, such as oil production companies, tend to have good asset value per share. On the other hand, labour intensive companies, computer servicing or advertising, for example, who do not need a lot of expensive equipment, can still make high profits. Consequently, their asset value per share may seem alarmingly low. This suggests that capital intensive companies have better fail-safe prospects in the event of trouble than labour intensive ones, and this is generally the case.

However, a company which uses a lot of very expensive machinery, may find that the liquidation value of its assets is much less than their original cost. If a particular business sector is in the process of change, the capital equipment it uses may suddenly become obsolescent. This is the reason why we need to use liquidation asset value rather than net asset value.

A famous example of over-estimated assets is to be found in the history of the United States railroad companies. They had invested enormous amounts of money on rolling stock and railway lines. The advent of air travel reduced the profitability of that capital to such an extent that many railroads went bankrupt even though they had enormous assets in the form or track and trains. Railway rolling stock is only of value to other railway companies, and when no one wants to travel by rail, its price falls to its scrap value.

The Investment Value of a Company

Liquidation value per share, when properly calculated, is a good measure of the 'worst case price' of a company's shares if that company should fail. However, it tells us nothing about the company's potential for success. It is no use asking the company itself about its earnings growth. Almost always, its ambitions for growth will be bigger than reality.

Just like individual humans, companies are often incurable optimists and, also like humans, the best way to predict their future performance is by paying attention to their past performance rather than their present promises. We can make an estimate of a company's future growth by using the figures for earnings growth over several past years. A company, which has failed to grow for the past five years, is unlikely to grow in the next five years no matter how optimistic the chairman might be.

Earnings growth is declared in a company's accounts, but the figures given there cannot always be accepted without modification. Companies are now obliged to separate out exceptional gains and losses. However it is wise to scrutinise closely how the earnings growth was achieved. Some care is needed and so we will discuss profit and loss accounts in the next chapter. Here it is necessary to note that growth in earnings is not the same as growth in dividends. A company may be using some of its earnings to finance its capital growth. In fact, for a growth company this will be the usual situation, and the company will not be borrowing money in order to expand. Consequently, its asset value will be increasing as well as its earnings.

If we want a really secure investment with modest returns, we can buy government bonds. So an investment in shares that are not going to do better than bonds, is a risk not worth taking. Why should we put ourselves at the mercy of Mr Market's mood swings, when we can buy government bonds and get fixed interest, paid on time, and our capital back when the bonds mature?

This is the criterion on which Warren Buffet bases his analysis strategy. We can compare a potential investment in any company with one in government bonds. This will give us the 'investment value' of the company, that is, the value to us as an alternative to investing in bonds. We can do this for several companies, and even though the value is only a rough estimate, it gives a means of comparing different companies, and finding ones which merit further investigation.

Consider a company, which we know to be growing its earnings at an average of, say 20% per year. Let's say that the earnings this year are 10p per share. Next year, if growth continues at 20%, the earnings will be 12p. If we can reasonably expect earnings to increase by 20% in the following few years, then the sequence of earnings projected five years into the future, will be 12, 14.4, 17.8, 20.7, 25. Taking the sum of these, we have total earnings of 89.9 p for five years, which is an average earnings of about 18p per year.

Assume for the purposes of this argument that government five year bonds have an interest rate of 9%. We can earn 18p per year for five years if we buy 200p worth of bonds. If the shares can be bought for 200p per share, there is no advantage in buying them since we can get just the same profit from the bonds with much more security. Note that all the earnings from the shares will not be received as dividends. Some of it will be retained inside the company to enable it to grow. However, these 'retained earnings' should eventually appear as increased asset value.

If we decide to buy the shares rather than the bonds, it is because we hope that in five years time, the shares will be worth more than the 200p we would get from redemption of the bonds. If we can buy the shares now, at less than 200p, then we are getting a better return than five year bonds. Any rise in the market price of the shares over the five years will be an added bonus - a reward for taking the risk of holding shares rather than bonds. It is not possible to calculate this reward precisely because of the unpredictable variation in market prices. However, in five years' time, if the company is still growing, we may not need to sell the shares anyway.

Calculating Investment Value

The simple rules for calculating the investment value of a particular growth share are as follows. Take the average earnings growth over the past five years, and use this to make predictions of earnings per share, in pence, for the next five years. Add up all the earnings for the five future years and divide it by five to get the average earnings per year over five years. Then take the interest rate (expressed as a decimal) on government five year bonds and divide this into the average earnings. This will give the investment value of the shares in pence.

Another example will make this clear. If shares in Growth Inc, are growing at 10% per annum, and the earnings per share this year is 10p, then the sequence of earnings for the next five years ought to be 11, 12.1, 13.3, 14.6, 16.1. The total earnings over five years is thus 67.2p and the average earnings per year will be 13.43p. If the interest rate on government five year bonds is 5%, the decimal equivalent of which is 0.05, then the investment value of the shares is $13.43/0.05 = 268.6$ per share.

We can calculate the investment value per share of any company if we know its growth record over a certain period, say five years, and assume that this can be projected into the future. We can use a shorter or longer period if we wish. In these days of rapid economic change, five years is probably the maximum we would want to look ahead. In fact, a shorter period of three years might, in some cases, be more appropriate, especially when trying out this method of analysis.

Once we have analysed a target company and established that its share price is at or below its investment value, we can then go on to investigate the likelihood that the company will be able to grow at the projected rate. This is part of what we will call the 'quality of business' of a company. In order to make an informed judgement on the sustainability of a company's growth pattern, we need to understand the company's business operations in some detail.

Quality of Business

A company which is growing will have a low dividend in percentage terms, partly because its share price is high and partly because it is retaining part of its earnings for internal investment. Therefore, the growth companies we wish to invest in will have a total return that is largely due to capital gain. By definition, therefore, a good company is one that grows steadily at a better-than-average rate. A bad company is one that declines, stands still, or just grows at a rate little better than inflation.

It is natural that in a dynamic economy new industries will be created as the old ones decline. One popular way to select investments is to buy shares in new business ventures. But that would be a mistake. Established businesses can always be made more profitable.

For example, the growth of supermarket shares has been powered almost entirely by increased efficiency in food marketing and supply. Food itself is not a growth product and demand is very stable, at least in volume. In contrast, we note that many new technologies are brought to commercial viability by small, start-up companies. This type of organisation is notoriously unstable and therefore very risky even though the market for its products is new and unexplored.

Warren Buffet is quite clear in choosing companies which he believes have some essence of monopoly about them. The absence of serious competition enables a company to push through price rises without having to worry about losing customers - so long as it does so at a moderate rate. This ensures that it can increase its revenue steadily, year after year, which is exactly what we are looking for. If it can do this at the same time as reducing its own costs and increasing its market share, then we have our ideal growth company. But a company which expands its turnover and its market share, yet does not increase its earnings, is going to a lot of trouble to stand still. Usually, this happens when a company is fighting against fierce competition, and this is not the sort of situation we want to invest in.

One of Buffet's best buys was Coca Cola. Though this company did not have a monopoly on soft drinks, it did have a very strong brand image. In certain circumstances this is almost as good as a monopoly. To understand why a brand image can act in this way it is only necessary to think of one's own reaction to certain products which have established themselves as unique items rather than one in a range. An extreme example is Rolls Royce motor cars. There are a variety of luxurious cars on the market, but by purchasing a Rolls we are buying an icon of luxury itself. Thus, it has a monopoly position in the market because of its uniqueness. A more mundane example is that of chocolate bars. Several of these are unique in taste, texture and wrapping, their brand image is distinct and well defined. We do not usually shop around for our favourite choc-bar, and habit, not cost, is the main reason why we buy the same brand year after year.

On the other hand, 'natural' monopolies, such as water, gas, and electricity companies, tend to be regulated by the government, and they find it difficult to push up prices too rapidly. Governments always say that they will limit increases in the price of utility services to the rate of inflation. Though they do not always keep this promise, the earnings growth of these companies is limited to what can be done with reducing input prices and operating costs.

The UK utilities, which were privatised in the 80s and 90s, have enjoyed substantial earnings growth over the few years that they have been in the private sector. This has been achieved largely by reducing costs. However, it is unlikely that they will be able to continue this growth record over the next five years.

Another indicator of an ideal growth company is that it has a good chance of cutting its costs, both operating costs and the cost of raw materials. A good example of companies that have grown earnings by these means has already been mentioned - the supermarkets. As already said, the demand for food is as steady as any market item can be, in quantity at least. Over the past thirty years, the supermarket chains have consistently increased their earnings. This has been done largely by pushing down wholesale prices and by introducing new technology in their stores, mainly the store layout, and electronic price checking at the tills.

It is not practicable to go through the economy discussing the companies in each individual sector. It must suffice to enunciate the two basic principles which Buffet and others have established as criteria for growth in earnings. These are as follows:

> i) a near monopoly position in the market and immunity from government regulation; and
>
> ii) some prospect of cost reduction through technology, and/ or input prices cuts.

Again, this is a simple list, and leaves out all sorts of special situations, such as take-over bids and mergers. However, we are looking for simple rules - anything more complicated would be more risky.

A Simple Analysis Method

We are now in a position to put together the main elements of a simple method of analysing a target company, and establish a set of rules. The

target company must be evaluated on the following three dimensions:
i) the investment value per share;
ii) the quality of the company's business; and
ii) the liquidation value per share.

The investment value per share is a rough estimate of the value of the company as an investment, over a certain time period, in comparison with government bonds of the same maturity. This is based on the company's growth record projected into the future. It's main virtue is that it enables companies to be compared with each other, and does not depend on market price.

How a company will perform in the future is not predictable with any certainty, but we can form an idea of its potential for success if we study the quality of its business. We should attempt to understand how it makes money and we should be able to see how it can increase earnings - which is the engine of capital growth.

The liquidation value gives us a measure of the 'margin of safety' that Graham advocates. It ensures that we don't get involved in enterprises with no assets, which can fail catastrophically. The liquidation value per share is the minimum share price we would expect if the company goes bust.

There are three main ways in which a company can increase its earnings:

i) increasing the prices of its products and services;
ii) reducing the cost of its inputs, i.e. labour and raw materials; and
iii) improvements in its technology which lead to higher productivity.

The depth of such a study depends on how much time, energy, and insight you have to put into your investments. However, I suggest that you at least stick to Warren Buffet's rule and do not invest in companies which you do not understand. Fortunately, most companies have a simple, secure way in which they generate their earnings, and this can easily be understood. But beware high-tech companies unless you have some special insights. Good technology may hide bad business.

Investing for Fun - Speculation

We can define the difference between investing and speculating in the following way. An investment is something we undertake with high expectations of making small profits, whereas speculation is something we undertake with small expectations of making high profits.

As an example, consider the following investment alternatives. Either we can invest in companies which have a 95% chance of success of making a 20% profit, or we can put money into projects which have a 10% chance of success for a 1040% profit. Which one we would choose depends on our nature even though, statistically, the gain is the same in each case.

What these figures do not show is that to win with low chances of success we need to make many ventures. The more often we take the high risk the sooner we reap the benefits of the averaging process. This is the essence of speculation - many short-term, high risk, but potentially very profitable, transactions. The few that succeed more than make up for the many that fail.

Even sensible people have an illogical attitude to risk. It seems that, in order to reverse a loss, people are willing to take risks which they would never take to make the same profit. Consider the following situation. You have been playing poker all evening and you are losing £100. When the game breaks up, the winner offers to let you win back your £100 by betting 'double or quits' on the toss of a coin. You are taking a 50% risk, for the chance of correcting a loss, and most people would do that.

On the other hand, if you were winning £100, and you were offered the same bet, you would probably turn it down. Why take a risk when you are winning anyway. The moral is that you should only gamble with money you can afford to lose, and if you lose it, don't be tempted to try to win it back by taking unacceptable risks.

Most people who have saved all their lives would be unwilling to commit those savings to a speculative venture. Those of us who crave excitement can always take up hang-gliding, bungee-jumping, or swimming in shark-infested seas. So speculating should be regarded as just another way of bringing a little excitement into life. Speculation is, in fact, very similar to swimming with sharks, in that it is possible to lose an arm or a leg before you even realise you are in danger. So what follows is a description of how it can be done, but definitely not a recommendation to try it.

Hedge funds originated when conventional investment funds began to use options and futures to 'hedge' their risk, which they did in order to protect the capital value of their assets. Some of these funds soon discovered that they could make more money using these hedging instruments than they could with their conventional investments. Instead of becoming more secure funds, as they originally intended, hedge funds became high risk ventures.

George Soros has been uniquely successful in this field. His success in predicting the rise and fall of asset prices and his use of options and futures to take advantage of price changes, has given his Quantum fund consistently high growth. George Soros is a very intelligent man who has made a life long study of market behaviour. His insights into the way markets boom and bust is at the heart of his trading strategy. He has identified the essential mechanism in market behaviour that makes it unstable, and he has used it to the advantage of his fund.

We discussed in an earlier chapter the fact that large investment funds can never buy or sell in a market without affecting the price. Mr Soros has turned this effect into a tool of his trade so that his intervention in a market with significant funds can precipitate a change in market sentiment. Of course, it is necessary to do this at critical times in order to succeed, but Soros has shown that his timing in doing this is very good.

The private investor cannot hope to match professional speculators in their mastery of the options and futures markets. However, he can make a profit if he has the time available to watch the markets and is able to take the stress of losing about as often as he gains. We have already discussed in a previous chapter how options on company shares can be traded on the London Stock Market. Options are a natural way for an investor in the same market to obtain a little excitement while waiting for his long term investments to mature.

All you have to do is identify shares that will rise or fall significantly in the short term, say, one to ten months. The money that can be lost is limited and the time scale of the process can be adapted to suit your life style. For example, if you are willing to spend all day watching prices change, then with a real-time data feed to your computer and a telephone readily available, you can trade several times a day, making perhaps a few percent profit or loss on each trade.

Option prices change continuously, and an alert trader can take advantage of these daily swings. On the other hand, if you just want to trade once a day, you do not need a real-time feed, and you can obtain delayed prices from the internet for a much more modest subscription. Again, trading on a weekly basis, making your decisions after reading the weekend newspapers, is another way of getting involved at even less cost, though with a longer time scale.

For those who like it hot, the futures market is even faster and more furious than options. Again, you can choose the time scale most convenient for you, from daily trading to weekly trading. The risks in futures are significantly higher than with options and you will need to deposit a 'margin' of several thousand pounds with your broker before he will let you open a trading account. You will also have to sign papers certifying that you are fully aware of the risks you are taking and can afford to lose the whole of your margin without financial distress.

This all sounds very serious, and it is. As we saw in chapter two, the losses you can incur trading futures, if the market goes against you, are without limit. Likewise, the potential gains are without limit, hence the increased excitement. It's here that sudden changes in market sentiment can leave you stranded in a losing position. Before you have realised what is happening, the trend has reversed and changed. Remember, Mr Soros is out there, he and the other professional speculators are fighting it out. If you get in their way your blood will not even be noticed in the swirl of frenetic feeding. On the other hand, it's equally probable that you may find yourself in a suddenly winning position. If a tasty morsel comes your way, you must be ready to snap it up, and run.

Chapter Six

Reading Company Accounts

Accounting for Company Business Operations

It is a legal requirement in most western economies, that a public company provides an annual report of its business operations, and that this must include an audited set of accounts. In the next chapter, we shall discuss financial information and how to obtain it. In this chapter, we will concentrate on the company accounts.

Company accounts must be presented to shareholders at an annual general meeting and the shareholders must approve the accounts. In addition, the validity of the accounts must be confirmed by a firm of accountants, who act as auditors. The format of the accounts is standardised and accounting procedures must conform to a strict code of practice. As things stand, it is very difficult for a company's managers to deceive both the shareholders and auditors, either as to the progress of the company or the state of its financial affairs. When companies fail, it is usually through failure to appreciate what is actually in the accounts rather than lack of accounting information.

In the previous chapter, we talked about the importance of understanding how a business makes its money. The annual accounts are a valuable insight into how the process works in detail, and it is important to have some knowledge of how accounting is done, and what the actual figures mean. Again, there is a lot of jargon that doesn't help the non-professional, but the principles of accounting are simple and sensible. Once these are grasped, we can begin to see what the vast array of numbers really mean.

Furthermore, we will be able to go quickly into a company's accounts and pluck out those few figures that are of importance to us.

Accounting for Income, Spending, and Assets Owned

Every company, like every man and woman, has income, expenditure, and owns some property. The golden rule that income must not fall below expenditure is familiar to us all in our daily lives, and this applies to companies in just the same way. In addition to keeping track of what we earn and what we spend, we also keep note of the value of our property. This may vary in value from year to year, even though this variation is unlikely to affect us unless we wish to sell that property. Again, the situation is exactly the same for a company. It has business income and expenses. Its property is the land, buildings, plant, and equipment it needs to conduct its business, the value of which is important only when it either buys new property or sells the old. Accounting is simply a formal way of declaring the details of company income and expenditure, and keeping track of the value of the company's property.

Most people know in detail how much they are earning and take care not to spend more than this amount. On the other hand, in a large public company it is difficult, on a day-to-day basis, to know both how much it is earning and how much it is spending. This is even more difficult when different departments are responsible for buying and selling. This information is vital for its business operations, and a company will take a lot of trouble to keep accurate, running estimates of income and expenditure. In addition, at the end of their financial year, the company draws together the annual totals of income and expenditure in the company report. This is known as the 'profit and loss' account.

The value of a person's property is not usually on his mind, unless, for example, his neighbours are selling their house. Then the price of his own house becomes interesting for a while. Likewise, for a company, the value of its property is of less concern, on a day-to-day basis, than income and expenditure. However, a realistic valuation of a company's assets is very important for the annual accounts since it is part of the formal, legal declaration of the company's asset value. The company 'balance sheet' is a valuation of all the assets of the company, 'balanced' against its liabilities. Unlike the profit and loss account, which is a record of activity covering the whole financial year, the balance sheet is a snap-shot valuation on the final day of its financial year.

The balance sheet is simply a list of all the company's assets - its liquid assets and property, and a list of all its liabilities - its loans and other financial commitments. Each asset and liability is assigned a valuation, and total asset value is set against total liability value, the 'balance' is the company's net asset value. This is sometimes called shareholders' funds, since it is this value of the asset that the shareholders actually own. If the company's assets have declined during the year, the shareholders will want to know how, and why. Again, for a large public company, which is constantly buying and selling plant and equipment, it is not easy to keep track of this property.

The profit and loss account, and the balance sheet are the two basic sources of information for the private investor investigating a company's performance. The rest of the company report consists of statements from various divisions of the company, its personnel, and its auditors. These other parts can give valuable insight into what the managers are doing and planning, but it is the accounts that present the unequivocal truth about the company. It is worthwhile, therefore, taking some time to understand what we are looking at, and what we are looking for.

Profit and Loss - The P&L Account

The profit and loss (P&L) account is essentially simple - it is only slightly more complicated than our own personal income and expenditure. A company provides products and/or services, for which it receives income.

In order to do this it must purchase raw materials, pay its staff, and replace any equipment worn out in the process - this is the company's expenditure. The difference between income and expenditure is the company's earnings. It is clear that money spent on maintaining equipment is a business expense and may be included in the P&L account since it represents a real expenditure. What is less obvious is that depreciation in the value of equipment and plant is also a legitimate business expense even though it does not represent money actually spent. Depreciation is a decrease in the valuation of property and therefore it must also be recorded on the balance sheet. The expenses of depreciation are effectively paid by the P&L account to the balance sheet. What the balance sheet records as a decrease in the value of an asset is compensated by an equivalent increase in the cash reserves.

A simple way to think of the profit and loss account is as the record of the input and output from a very large petty cash box. During the year, the company finances its business operations from the cash in the box. At the end of the year, any extra cash is paid out as dividends or transferred to the balance sheet. If the company makes a loss, and the amount in the box is negative, then it must be made good by transfers from the balance sheet. The basic layout of a Profit and Loss Account is shown right.

This contains all the basic ingredients of a typical account. In addition to income from the sale of its goods and services, the company may also receive income from other sources. An example is the interest the company receives if it has money in the bank. The company may make an exceptional profit if it sells some of its assets at above the valuation recorded in the balance sheet - their 'book value'. These 'special items' must be recorded in the profit and loss account.

Expenditure is simply the cost of raw material, the operating cost of transforming it to saleable products, and special items. An example of special items is the interest paid on bank loans, or a loss made when assets are sold off at less than their book value. A more usual special item is bad debt and provision for bad debt.

The sale of goods and services is often conducted on a credit basis; that is, the customer has a certain period of time in which to pay. The profit and loss account assumes that the money has been paid, and the value of payments which remains outstanding is recorded in the balance sheet under the heading 'debtors'. If the customer is eventually unable to pay then the debt must be written off as a 'bad debt' and accounted for as a business expense. Usually, bad debts are, to a limited extent, predictable, and a company is able to make provisions for failure to pay long before the debtor defaults. So 'provision for bad debt' is another business expense recorded in the profit and loss account.

Capital and Labour

Different types of companies will have different levels of the items shown in the profit and loss account. For example, a motor car manufacturing company which uses a lot of expensive machinery, will have large depreciation, maintenance, and fuel costs, as well as large costs for raw materials.

However, even though it employs many workers, their contribution per unit of sales is quite small because the average number of cars produced by each worker in one year is quite high.

On the other hand, workers in an advertising agency make a large contribution to sales since much of the work is labour intensive and requires few raw materials. Such a company will require little in the way of machinery and so its depreciation, maintenance and fuel costs will be low.

This suggests a classification of companies as being labour intensive or capital intensive. At one end of this scale are the so-called heavy industries which need lots of expensive machinery, at the other are the service industries which use little capital equipment but lots of labour. The ratio of maintenance and depreciation costs to labour costs is a good indicator of a company's position on this scale.

The Classic Balance Sheet

The P&L account records actual cash transactions, and there is usually no doubt about the numbers thus recorded. On the other hand, the balance

Profit and Loss Account for Typical PLC	
Income	
Sales of Goods & Services	£ 100,000
Special Items	£ 10,000
Total	**£110,000**
Expenditure	
Raw Materials	£ 10,000
Operating Costs	
Wages	£ 10,000
Fuel	£ 10,000
Maintenance	£ 10,000
Depreciation	£ 10,000
Total	**£ 40,000**
Special Items	**£ 10,000**
Total	**£ 60,000**
Profit	**£ 50,000**
Dividends	**£ 30,000**
Transfer to Reserves	**£ 20,000**

sheet is about valuations and this allows a large margin of subjectivity to creep in. It is here that errors are most easily made and where company fraud is most commonly committed.

Valuing assets is an imprecise art, and it is not difficult for a company to deceive itself, as well as others, as to the value of its property. It is important to realise that there is no certain way to know what something is worth except by actually selling it. In fact, a good definition of 'value' is simply 'price paid', and until that price is actually paid, no one can say for certain the value of anything.

The assets of a company are of two basic kinds, 'current assets' and 'fixed assets'. A current asset is either cash or something that can be sold quickly for cash, for example, shares in another company. Fixed assets are buildings, land, plant and equipment, intellectual property such as patents and copyrights, and brand image. The negative of an asset is called a 'liability' and again these are of two kinds, loans of money to the company, and commitments to buy goods or services. A typical balance sheet is shown on the previous page.

The Company's assets which are tangible, that is, can be seen and counted, are mainly the property it occupies and the machinery it uses. The only doubts about this are the valuations. Its intangible assets are patent rights, contracts and brand image. Patent rights have commercial value, not just because of the royalties paid by others to use them, but also in stopping their competitors using them. Contracts may also have asset value, particularly for long term supply of goods and services. Brand image is also listed as an asset, even thought it is difficult to define and has no legal validity other than the copyright of a name or a logo. This may include what used to be called customer 'good will', that is, the tendency for customers to make repeat purchases.

Current assets are those assets which can be disposed of quickly, hence the name used in the United States, 'quick assets'. These are the reserves,

Classical Balance Sheet for Typical PLC

Assets
Fixed Assets

Property	£1,000,000
Machinery	£1,000,000
Patents	£ 100,000
Contracts	£ 100,000
Brands	£ 100,000
Total	**£2,300,000**

Current Assets

Reserves	£ 100,000
Debtors	£ 10,000
Stocks	
Unsold	£ 10,000
Materials	£ 10,000
Total	**£ 130,000**
Total Assets	**£2,430,000**

Liabilities
Capital

Shares	£2,000,000
Bonds	£ 400,000
Total	**£2,400,000**

Current Liabilities

Bank loan	£ 10,000
Creditors	£ 10,000
Contracts	£ 10,000
Total	**£ 30,000**

held as money in the bank, money owed by debtors, and stocks of raw material and unsold stock. Reserves include money that is taken from the profit and loss account for depreciation of assets. The total asset value does not change because the same amount is deducted from the value of the corresponding assets. Reserves may be held in other forms, gilts, stocks and shares of other companies, short term loans to the money market etc. Money owed by debtors is more problematical since it may not be recoverable. Stocks are again a difficult area. Supplies of raw materials are usually saleable. Unsold stock is valued as cost, though sometimes it may be unsaleable.

Liabilities are divided into two categories, those to do with the original money subscribed as capital to the company, and the other liabilities.

When a company is set up, shares are sold and the proceeds form the capital of the company. Sometimes bonds are issued in addition, and these also go to form the capital base of the company. There is no obligation on the company to return payment to shareholders except as dividends, but bonds are issued with a promise of redemption at a given date in the future. However, shares are treated as an obligation, though it is not the same as the promise made to the bond holders.

A company can also obtain money via a bank loan, and the payment of interest is a legitimate company expense and appears in the profit and loss account. The company's suppliers may give credit, and this is an obligation that must be recorded in the balance sheet. Finally, some contracts should be considered as liabilities. For example, an obligation to make severance payments to directors if they leave before their service contract expires. In addition, some long term supply contracts may turn out to be a liability if the price of goods and services change unexpectedly.

This way of laying out a balance sheet shows clearly the original input of capital from the shareholders and bondholders. However, as time passes, and assets are bought and sold, and profits accumulate or losses are made

Shareholders' Balance Sheet for Typical PLC

Assets

Fixed Assets
Tangible Assets

Property	£1,000,000
Machinery	£1,000,000

Intangible Assets

Patents	£ 100,000
Contracts	£ 100,000
Brands	£ 100,000

Total	**£2,300,000**

Current Assets

Reserves	£ 100,000
Debtors	£ 10,000

Stocks

Unsold	£ 10,000
Materials	£ 10,000

Total	**£ 130,000**

Total Assets	**£2,430,000**

Liabilities
Long term liabilities

Contracts	£ 10,000
Bonds	400,000

Total	**£ 410,000**

continued

good with bank loans, this way of showing the balance of assets and liabilities is too complicated. Company accounts usually use a different format that shows more clearly the balance of shareholders' funds.

Shareholders' Funds

For the purposes of making clear how assets and liabilities are balanced, the format below is used.

Short term liabilities	
Bank	
Overdraft	£ 10,000
Creditors	£ 10,000
Total	**£ 20,000**
Total Liabilities	**£ 430,000**
Shareholders' Funds **(Assets less Liabilities)**	**£2,000,000**

This way of laying out the balance sheet is similar to a profit and loss account. The phrase 'shareholders' funds' does not imply that there is an amount of cash equal to this value. They are in the form of assets, and are simply what's left over when net liabilities are deducted from net assets. This is also the asset value of the company as a going concern.

Exceptional Profits and Losses

The profit and loss account should give an accurate picture of how the company makes money. Basically, the company charges for the goods and services it supplies, and pays the costs of providing these goods and services. To make money the company must charge more than its costs. On this simple level, it is usually clear when a company is making a loss or a profit. However, the existence of assets and liabilities that are continually being acquired and disposed of, and the changes in value of these, can obscure the essential clarity of the profit and loss account. The financial effects of these changes are recorded in the profit and loss account and come under the heading 'other items'.

The balance sheet records the annual valuation of all the company's assets. While these assets remain with the company, they are carried in the balance sheet at their theoretical valuation (book value), but when the company disposes of them, their value is realised as a price paid. A problem arises when the valuation and the price differ by a large amount. For example, a fleet of transport vehicles may have cost £100,000, and in the year they are purchased they appear on the balance sheet at this value. Each year thereafter, the company deducts an amount from their value to account for depreciation. This is charged as a business expense and is transferred to the reserves. However, when the company finally replaces the vehicles, it may find that it has been too pessimistic in its valuation of the vehicles, and it may get more for them than the current book value. The extra money is an exceptional profit, and must be recorded in the profit and loss account. What has happened is that, in the past, the company charged too much depreciation and this exceptional profit is simply profit from previous years that went unrecognised.

The more usual situation is when a company charges too little depreciation, and when it disposes of the corresponding asset, it gets less than the book value. This is an exceptional loss, and it is really accumulated losses that were unrecognised in previous years. This kind of situation can be much more serious when assets depreciate suddenly, for example, when new technology makes existing equipment obsolete. Even if the equipment is not to be sold off, the company sometimes acknowledges its sudden depreciation by 'writing off' some of its value on the balance sheet.

Write-offs

'Write-offs' are necessary when balance sheet valuations have to be adjusted quickly. Companies usually try to keep asset valuations and depreciation as near to reality as possible. However, it is difficult, and even with the best will in the world, it cannot be done perfectly. Of course, when a company is in trouble, these valuations are often used as a way of disguising the extent of the problem.

The balance sheet may give a misleading picture in many ways. One of them is through over-estimation of assets. Two items that frequently occurs on the balance sheet are 'work in progress' and 'unsold stock'. In a manufacturing company, goods which are still in the process of being made on valuation day, are listed as 'work in progress'. The stock of finished goods which have yet to be sold are put down as 'unsold stock'. Valuing these might seem easy, and in many cases it is. However, a large quantity of unsold stock may indicate that the stock is, in reality, unsaleable. In a situation of this kind, valuing the finished and unfinished stock in the usual way would be misleading.

Purchasing Assets - Capital formation

The company's earnings are used to pay dividends to the shareholders and to augment the company's assets. A growing company will usually need to buy new equipment, and it is usual to do this out of its own earnings if at all possible. Money spent on new equipment disappears from the cash reserves and appears as asset value in the balance sheet.

If a company does not have enough cash reserves to buy new equipment it can borrow from the bank, issue bonds or preference shares, or issue new ordinary shares. The consequence of borrowing, either from the bank or via bonds or preference shares, is that interest has to be paid on the loan and this is an extra charge against future earnings. If new shares are issued, then future profits have to be shared amongst more shares. Therefore, it is better for the shareholders if growth can be financed out of earnings, even if it means accepting lower dividends for a while.

This process of new investment by existing companies is called capital formation and it is the main way in which new capital is created. A company which can do this without borrowing or issuing new shares will grow its net asset value, which is a good thing. If a company has to borrow in order to finance growth, then the extra liabilities on the balance sheet will reduce the increase in assets. In the worst cases, the increased liabilities become greater than the increase in assets and the company has effectively shrunk its asset base, even though it may have increased production

Hidden Assets and Liabilities

Since assets must be purchased it is difficult to hide them. A hidden asset is simply an old asset that has risen in value but which is not recorded at its proper value on the balance sheet. This usually happens with land, but it can happen with other assets, such as patents, which suddenly become more valuable as technology progresses. Increases in asset values appear as extra income in the profit and loss account even though the company does not receive any money. Thus they may produce extra profits which are taxable, and therefore, there is a reluctance to acknowledge them.

The problem in the 1990s has been one of hidden liabilities. This usually occurs when a company signs a contract to buy goods or services that it eventually does not need. A spectacular example was the contract that the former British Gas company signed to buy gas at a price that subsequently proved too high. At the time of signing, it seemed a good deal, but as gas prices fell, the contract became a liability rather than an asset.

More recent examples of hidden liabilities are the contracts that some companies sign to employ their senior managers. These often have very generous bonus and severance payments and should be recorded on the company balance sheet. A similar situation occurs with share options.

This costs money even though it is the shareholders who pay because their holding is diluted.

Liquidation Asset Value

The asset value of a company, as stated in its balance sheet, is a reasonable estimate of the value that the company places on itself as a going concern. It is not the price that would be paid for the company's property if it failed and was put into 'liquidation'. To find what that is we would have to wait for the liquidator to sell the company as a whole or in parts. However, we can make a reasonable estimate by looking into the balance sheet and eliminating certain items that would be worthless in the event of company failure.

The most obvious of these is brand image. When a company fails, this disappears. Another example is the value of large specialist machines and the buildings which have been constructed to house them. If the company cannot be sold as a going concern it indicates that this production capacity is not needed and therefore the plant is worthless, or even a liability. The blast furnaces in the old steel works are a case of this. Another is the pit-head equipment in coal mines.

Take-over Value

When a company is doing business and making money, its assets are said to be 'employed' and, as such, command a far higher price than if they become 'unemployed'. We only really find out what a company is worth as a going concern when it is taken over, and take-over prices are usually very much in excess of asset value.

However, in normal circumstances, the share price of a company is the market price, that is, the price of a small number of shares. It's only when a buyer wants to buy all the shares that he has to bid up the price to take-over value.

The market share price of a company multiplied by the number of shares in issue is known as the capital value of the company. It is a common phenomenon that the share price will increase dramatically when it is known that a company is the subject of a take-over bid. When a company is taken over, its capital value rises to its take-over value, and since it is a price paid, can be regarded as a real value. On the other hand, when a company is put into liquidation its component parts are put up for sale. Then its capital value falls to its liquidation asset value, which since it is a price paid, is also a real value.

Invisible Assets

Every company has staff, and almost every company makes declarations in its annual report that its staff are its most valuable asset. However, the quality or otherwise of a company's staff is not recorded on the balance sheet either as an asset or a liability. Clearly staff loyalty is important but it is difficult to see how it can be valued since most of the company's employees are free to leave at short notice.

This is particularly a problem for companies which are labour intensive and where the staff are highly trained. Staff loyalty in such companies is clearly a very important asset. The company's profitability is due entirely to their skill, and not to expensive machinery. For sporting organisations, like football clubs, this is a serious problem. It has been partly solved by persuading key players to sign contracts for several years at a time. This is expensive, but it gives the club some assurance that their invisible assets will not walk away to play for their rivals. Other kinds of companies with key staff do the same thing, and these contracts are a form of asset. However, the majority of companies have no such contracts, and staff loyalty, which exists and is important, cannot adequately be valued.

Brand image, like staff loyalty, is another important feature of a company that can make the difference between profit and loss. The value of a company's image or reputation used to be recorded in the balance sheet as 'good will' since its benefit was deemed to derive from the good will of the company's customers. Perhaps a better name would have been 'customer loyalty', but with the advent of advertising on a huge scale, the phenomenon now has the name 'Brand Image'.

Companies spend a lot of money on advertising to maintain their brand image. This is similar to capital investment, in that the effects of advertising last much longer than the period of promotional spending.

In the last chapter we saw how a strong brand image allowed a company to behave as a quasi-monopoly. A brand image is a very powerful force to have working for you, and it is obviously of value, though this is not recorded on the balance sheet.

Cash Flow and Capital Structure

The profit and loss account and the balance sheet contain all that is financially true of a company. However, since money charged to depreciation does not leave the company, and assets written off do not result in actual money being paid out, the amount of cash the company has is not clear from looking at the two main accounts.

The cash flow statement tells directly the amount of cash in the company and how this has changed from the previous year. On a long term basis, it is value which counts, but in the short term, cash flow is vitally important. For a company to be short of cash means it has to borrow from the bank, and this can be expensive. In contrast, a large build-up of cash may make a company vulnerable to take-over.

The capital structure of a company shows how the company was originally set-up and how it has been modified during its lifetime. Each class of share is authorised to be issued up to a certain number. If there are still shares unissued then the company can use these to raise funds. The problem for existing shareholders is that the new shares 'dilute' their own holdings.

For example, if the company doubles the number of shares in issue, then each existing shareholder's share of the company's assets is halved. Of course, the money from the share sale increases the company's assets, but this is cash which has a tendency to disappear quickly.

The existence of preference shares, bonds, and warrants will also be noted as part of capital structure. The date of redemption of bonds and preference shares will be given together with the interest being paid, the number in issue, and the terms of conversion for convertible preference shares. Warrants are options to buy shares at a certain price at a given future date. They are a quick way to raise money, and again they can dilute share-holdings if the warrants are exercised and new shares have to be issued. The asset value of a company may look good on the balance sheet, but the existence of preference shares and warrants may dilute it in the near future. Their issue usually indicates that the company has been in financial trouble in the past and it is as well to find out why.

Limitations to Company Accounts

In trying to form an impression of a company's value, the private investor can read the company's accounts. However, this gives only a limited picture of how the company really works and what its value is from various stand points. It is an internal view, and it should be supplemented by comment from newspapers and other unbiased sources.

Since we do not want to invest in companies which are near to failure, we do not need to dwell too long on working out the company's liquidation value. We have already discussed which assets we can include and which ought to be excluded.

The main account item we really need to estimate with some accuracy is earnings and earnings growth. Again, we have discussed this and seen that some exceptional items need to be excluded, and others included, even though it may be necessary to backdate them. It is worthwhile taking some time to do this with care, because growth is the important factor we are searching for. Because of exceptional items in the profit and loss account, growth needs to be assessed over a number of years. Five years is a reasonable period to use. The actual growth rate is best calculated as an average too.

Given a growth record, then it is possible to calculate 'investment' value of the company on a five year growth projection. However, the validity of this valuation is critically dependent on the growth continuing on the expected trajectory. No figures in the company accounts will give you any guarantee that future growth will be the same as past growth. Only a detailed knowledge of the company and the way it works can provide this assurance.

The company report gives a lot of financial information about the company and the views of management. If you look at past reports you can see how the views of management change. Since consistency is what we most value in management, any shifting of ground or equivocation, is a bad sign.

However, since we will be looking for just a few companies for our portfolio, we can afford to be choosy. With a portfolio of, say, ten different companies, with an average life of four or five years each, we need to identify only two or three companies per year. If we limit ourselves to investigating one company per week, this gives us a hit ratio of 1 in 25. Even then, we might not want to buy the company's shares if the price is too high. So over a period of several years it is wise to compile a list of companies which fulfil the criteria we have discussed to qualify as growth companies. As share prices move up and down, the chance will come to buy these shares at a reasonable price.

Remember Benjamin Graham's dictum - buy good shares on bad days.

Chapter Seven

Financial Information: Finding it and using it.

News and Opinion

There is no shortage of financial information. Our task is not so much to find it as to filter it. We live in an information age, and knowing what is going on is not the problem that it used to be. Ignoring the information we do not need is now more difficult than finding the data we do need.

The swirls and eddies of world events create news continuously, but the flow is not steady, it fluctuates from day-to-day. In contrast, the media coverage of news in pages and hours is more or less constant. Thus the available news is expanded or shrunk to conform to the average daily template, and it is a task of the journalist to perform this fitting operation.

The situation with financial events and the corresponding flow of news is slightly more favourable. Markets are open at given times for fixed periods and the flow of prices generated by the markets can usually be packaged in more or less fixed space. However, it is important to realise that when news is in short supply, the deficiency is usually filled up with opinion. In addition, commentators have to comment on the news no matter how much or little comments are called for.

Financial journalism is not an easy profession, it has to report day after day, fill so many column inches, pack in facts when they are in abundance and pad them out when they are not. Financial journalists are usually, skilled, reliable and serious people. However, they would not wish to be relied on for investment advice, nor to be held accountable for opinions expressed perhaps in the heat of the moment, which later prove unfair or unfounded.

As an independent investor you are responsible for your own decisions, and separating news from views, and hard fact from personal opinion is something that you have to learn to do for yourself. It is wise to be an active news gatherer rather than a passive news absorber. This task is difficult because there is so much news and data available, and sifting the wheat from the chaff can take time.

The sources of financial news are manifold, ranging from annual company reports, monthly and weekly magazines and television programmes, daily newspapers, internet sites, and specialist providers of real-time prices via TV or satellite broadcasting.

In choosing which ones to use, it is necessary to decide how deeply you want to be involved. The minimum level for a private investor is to read a financial newspaper two or three times a week. For those with more time available, a computer with internet facilities will provide access to on-line databases of company information and price histories. Buying access to real time prices is not recommended unless you want to be involved in buying and selling on a daily basis.

This chapter describes some of these media and tries to rate them according to their usefulness to the independent investor. We also discuss strategies for reading and finding information.

Company Reports

All shareholders on a company's share register must be sent a copy of its annual report. In addition, the company is willing, and often keen, to send a copy to anyone who asks for it. All you have to do is telephone the head office and ask for a copy, they will take your name and address and a copy will arrive in the post within a few days. You do not even have to pay the postage.

To find the company's telephone number, you can ask directory enquiries, or look them up in a company directory such as the one published by Hemmington Scott. If you have a computer and a connection to the internet, then you can access Hemmington Scott's internet site. This site contains addresses, telephone numbers, and some brief financial details on a large number of public companies.

Assuming you have obtained the latest annual report of a company that you are analysing, the first thing you should realise is that the inform-ation may be more or less out of date. The accounts will be for the company's last financial year, and the report is not made available until a few months after the end of that year. So check the date of the year-end to which the report relates. This is given on the accounts page.

Some companies issue an interim report, a sort of half-time score, and this may be more relevant. In addition, there may be 'company statements' which are issued when significant new information has to be publicly reported. You can obtain interim reports and statements from the company head office and it is well to check if any are available when you ask for the annual report.

The profit and loss account and the balance sheet are always to be found in the annual report. They are clearly labelled as such, and even though the actual accounts may be encrusted with notes, the essential information we need for analysing the company is clearly stated. The notes are helpful if you need to delve into the details of some financial aspect of the company.

After the accounts, the most important part worth reading is the Chairman's statement. This will explain what the company achieved over the year, how it exceeded its targets or why it missed them. It will note market conditions and make predictions about next year's performance. It is as well to realise that this is a statement of opinion, albeit, the chairman's opinion - which may or may not be better than anyone else's.

Other managers may be allowed to have their say in the report, which can give you a lot of detail about the company's operations. It is here that you will find information to help you understand how the company makes money, and what the managers think about what they are doing in the company. If there is a good story to be told, the report will tell it. If the story is not a good one, then you will have to surmise it for yourself.

The difficulty is that the company report almost always tells a good story. It's up to you to assess its credibility. If what they are saying seems unlikely, then start looking for the bad news.

The report also contains statements about company cash flow, capital structure, and remuneration of directors and other staff. This is well worth reading too. Cash flow seems a strange thing to report on, but companies which are asset rich and cash poor may find themselves suddenly in trouble if their cash flow dries up. The cash flow statement tells you, without equivocation, the increase or decrease in cash over the year.

The capital structure will tell you how many shares the company has in issue and how many more it could issue if it wanted to. This is important, because if the company needs cash, it may decide to issue more shares and this will affect the price of shares already in the market. It will also tell you about any preference shares in issue, and the terms under which they can be converted or redeemed.

Perhaps the most interesting section is the remuneration of managers and staff. Here you can see what the managers pay themselves for running the company. It is now customary for managers to be given share options, which are also listed in the company report. Remember, the cost of these options often falls directly on the shareholders.

To invest in a company without having read its annual report is a reckless act. It is like buying a house without making a proper survey. Of course, most of the time you will not buy into disaster, but the risk that you might is just not worth taking when it is so easy to obtain the report. It will not tell you everything you want to know, at least, not explicitly. However, what it does contain is the legal truth about the company, and what is not said directly, can often be surmised by the naturally suspicious private investor.

The financial press - what to look for

Financial data is reported extensively, it consists of numbers - share prices, traded volume, etc, and it is very specific. Unfortunately, it exists in vast quantities and there is no way that it can be absorbed in its raw, numerical format. Charts or graphs are a good way of visualising how this information changes over time. The financial press often give charts to illustrate the news, and if you are not familiar with this way of visualising information, it is well worthwhile taking time to learn how to read them.

However, the most useful information in the financial press is the news and comment. Again, it exists in vast quantities, but the nature of news as stories means that we can absorb it much more easily. Nevertheless, it is impossible to take in the whole of one day's edition of a paper like the Financial Times or the Wall Street Journal. So it is necessary to be selective.

A wise investor keeps a list of the companies in which he would like to invest when the price is right. A file on each, containing company reports and news articles, is easy to refer to and update. The problem is that if you only read about the companies you are interested in, then you will miss out on adding interesting companies to that list. Therefore, a good strategy for reading will be to monitor existing interests in detail, and to scan all other articles searching for new ones.

Existing interests will also include the list of companies whose shares you hold. For the companies already in your portfolio, you need to look at the share price and check that it hasn't fallen to more than 10% of its previous high. If it has, then you need to find out why. We have discussed how this is done in chapter six, and it is for this purpose that we need to look at stock indexes and evaluate the global 'financial climate'.

You may also want to check the various financial indicators on a daily basis. The basic set is stock index values, interest rates, inflation rate, and exchange rate. These will rise and fall in a way which defies rational expectations, nevertheless, the paper will always have some explanation or comment. These need not be taken too seriously. The main reason for monitoring the 'financial climate' is to be ready when prices fall to the level where there might be good buying opportunities.

The task of searching for companies to add to your interested list is not so straightforward. The criteria we outlined in chapter five are that the company should have good growth, reasonable asset backing and a good business operation. Companies in the headlines will not usually be there for any of these reasons, so it is necessary look deeper than the story line.

Each day there will be several company news stories, as you read them ask yourself the question - is this a good business to be in. If the answer is yes, then obtain a company report and look deeper. The number of companies we need to invest in is quite small, so the statistics are on our side. We can afford to be choosy, and if we only need three or four companies per year, looking at one per week, in depth, should give us plenty of choice.

There are many newspapers and almost all employ a financial journalist to comment on the news. Every day there are many companies in the news, and many commentators' opinions. The popular press is just as good a place to find target companies, though the specialist press will cover a wider range.

Two great newspapers that specialise in this field, are the Financial Times in Europe, and the Wall Street Journal in north America. Their coverage of financial data is so comprehensive that it is worth explaining it in some detail.

The Financial Times

This famous pink paper is the most prolific source of financial information in Europe. Each day it publishes the end-of-day prices and other details of a wide range of financial instruments quoted on the London markets, as well as summary information from financial centres around the world. In particular, it has official end-of-day prices for all the shares in public companies traded on the London Stock Exchange, and all its own FT indices, of which the FTSE100 is the most famous.

The financial news is covered well, and the other news is treated soberly and sensibly, lacking the sensationalism of conventional newspapers. The FT has been a pioneer of financial bench-marking and reporting for several decades, and its position as a world leader is richly deserved. It now publishes an international edition, so if you buy it abroad be prepared to see a somewhat different format than the one you are familiar with.

There are several thousand companies whose share prices are quoted on the LSE, and their end-of-day prices are printed in the FT on the following morning. The price given is a 'mid' price, that is, an average of the bid and offer prices at the close of trading. In addition, five other pieces of information are given under column headings, as follows.

+ or -	the change on the previous days price
52 week high/low	the high/low share price over the last 52 weeks
Volume in 000s	the total number of shares traded in thousands
Yield Gross	the last declared annual dividend as a percentage before tax
P/E	the ratio of share price to annual earnings

The companies are listed according to economic activity, and there are 39 separate groups, from Alcoholic Beverages to Water Companies. Each of these groups has an index that represents a measure of price level in that particular sector. This is part of the FT system of indices of UK economic activity.

FT Indices

In addition to publishing the end-of-day prices of a wide range of individual financial instruments, the FT has also devised a range of indices (or indexes). Indices provide a way of indicating the price level of a whole market, or market sector, in contrast to that of its individual components. An index of a market is simply an average of the prices quoted in that market, but because these prices are not equally significant, they are 'weighted' in the averaging process according to the size of the company.

An index can be used to 'bench-mark' the performance of an individual company, that is, the change in a company's share price can be compared with the change in the relevant index over the same period. For example, you might find that a target company has increased its share price by 25% over the past year. This seems impressive, but if the relevant index also increased by the same amount then the company's performance was just average. On the other hand, if the company's shares fell by 10% and the index fell by 25%, then the company actually out performed the index by 15%, which is good.

The FTSE100 index is a weighted average of share prices of the 100 largest capital value public companies traded on the LSE. (The 'capital value' of a company is simply the share price multiplied by the number of shares in issue. This figure varies from day-to-day with the share price, and is an indicator of a company's size).

The weighting of share prices in the FTSE100 is according to each company's capital value. The average is therefore proportional to the total capital value of all the companies in the FTSE100.

A similar weighted average is also calculated for the second top 250 companies, known as the Mid-250, and another one for the rest of the stocks traded, called EX-350. The index representing a weighted average of all companies quoted on the LSE is known as the FT-All-Share. These four indices are calculated for end-of-day prices and published in the FT on the following day.

There are also variants of these indices for high and low yield companies, and for non-information technology companies.

The FT has classified the UK economy into several sectors and it publishes indices for each. The 39 groups of companies are further classified as follows:

- Financials;
- Non-Financials -
    Resources,
    General Industrial,
    Consumer Goods,
    Services,
    Utilities;
- Investment Trusts.

This way of looking at the economy is useful, since most factors that affect the performance of a company in one sector will also affect other companies in the same sector. It may even be that one sector of the economy is in recession while others are not. This phenomenon can help you to identify sectors from which to select companies for analysis.

Investment Trusts are given a separate index of their own. Since their asset value is made up entirely of shares of other companies, their capital value is already counted in the capitalisation of the other companies in the other sectors. In addition, the FT gives slightly different daily data for Investment Trusts than for the other companies.

Again, as well as the price, there are five extra pieces of information, given under column headings as follows:

+ or -	the change on the previous days price
52 week high/low	the high/low share price over the last 52 weeks
Yield Gross	the last declared annual dividend as a percentage before tax
NAV	Net Asset Value per share
Dis or Prem (-)	the price discount (or premium) to the asset value per share, as a percentage.
Negative value	indicates a premium

FT Bonds and Foreign Currencies

As well as shares, the FT publishes the prices of all UK Government Bonds (Gilts) in issue. At any one time there are nearly one hundred, each with a different maturity and yield. The listing gives the previous day's price in five columns of data as follows

Int	running yield (effective interest rate)
Red	redemption yield
Price £	price in pounds Sterling
+ or -	the change on the previous days price
52 week high/low	the high/low price over the last 52 weeks

There are also end-of-day prices for the government bonds of twenty industrialised countries around the world, as well as some for emerging economies.

The FT gives a matrix of exchange rates for 17 currencies. In addition, it gives the market details for trading of Sterling and the US dollar against 38 currencies together with their 'forward' rates, that is, the projected exchange rate, for one month, three months, and a year.

Wall Street Journal

The Wall Street Journal is the American equivalent of the Financial Times. It contains information on world financial instruments with a focus on north America. It reports financial news and world news, again with a focus on north America.

The main financial information is the closing prices of the three main north American stock markets, Wall Street (the New York Stock Exchange), NASDAQ, and the American Stock Exchange. This covers more than six thousand companies in north America. Some large companies from the rest of the world are included amongst these, but the prices are quoted in dollars and the shares appear as ADR - American Depository Receipts. These are packages of the shares specially issued for the American market.

The New York Stock Exchange, which has about 3,000 companies, is covered in most detail. The listing gives ten pieces of information for each stock. These are:
- 52 week high and low;
- dividend in cents;
- percentage yield;
- price/earnings ratio;
- daily volume in 100s;
- day's high and low;
- day's close;
- change on the day.

NASDAQ, which has about 2,000 companies, is given less coverage, with only five pieces of data, as follows:
- daily high and low;
- daily volume;
- closing price;
- daily change.

The American Stock Exchange, which consists of less than 1000 stocks, is covered with even less detail, giving only the closing price and the daily change.

Similar coverage is given to a few hundred stocks from the Toronto stock market. The daily closing data from the main companies in 18 European stock markets are given, these include Turkey and South Africa. Asian stocks are covered by a list of the main companies from the exchanges in Japan, Australia, Singapore and Hong Kong.

There is also daily data for Index Options, Stock Options, and Futures. The daily data for trading in US bonds, of which there are several hundred, is given in detail. Currency cross exchange rates are listed for 18 world currencies, and exchange rates for the dollar against the currencies of over 50 countries are given.

The main indexes quoted are those prepared by Dow Jones, a company which specialises in indexing a wide variety of financial instruments. The most well known is the Dow Jones Industrial Index (DJI), but there are many others, covering most financial centres in the world. The Index Options market uses the DJ indices.

The Wall Street Journal is a very readable paper, its comments are topical and the information is invaluable to anyone with financial interests in north America. The paper is in two sections, one for data and the other for news and comment. There are many graphs and blocks of summary data and, even for European investors, is well worth reading occasionally.

Information on the Internet

If you have a computer, it is a simple and inexpensive matter to obtain a connection to the internet via your telephone line. This is a world wide information network accessible over a telephone line by running a special programme known as an internet 'browser'. This is a very user-friendly interface that allows you to download information from internet 'sites'. The browser allows you to find and access information sources with minimum of skill and inconvenience.

There are many sites which supply financial information, some are free whilst some require you to register and pay a fee. Generally, a small fee is worthwhile since it gives you unlimited access to a vast array of information. For specialised and real time information the fee can be quite substantial.

The most useful free service for UK investors is perhaps the Hemmington Scot site. This has data on all the UK public companies. It is quick and easy to use. The data is summary financial information, share price graphs, contact information, major shareholder listings, and brokers consensus expectations. During market opening hours, it also provides a share price quotation delayed by 15 minutes.

The FT home page is an internet version of the FT daily paper. All the main stories are there plus the share prices that would appear in that day's FT. It is free, all you have to do is register. The Wall Street Journal has a similar service but it requires you to pay a small subscription. Most newspapers have free internet sites, and these give you access to their financial news and comments pages.

End-of-day, and Near Real-Time Price Data

There are hundreds of internet companies which provide financial information in large quantities. It is here that you can find price/time charts of almost all the financial instruments and economic indicators that you will be likely to find of interest. Most of these companies are based in north America and charge subscriptions. The two most useful in Britain are Datastream and UpData.

Datastream: This service gives prices of LSE shares delayed by 20 minutes. It also has some simple charts, and an archive of news stories. It is a subscription service.

135

UpData: This service gives prices of LSE shares as real time quotes or delayed by ten minutes. There is a report section. Subscription depends on the level of service.

Both of these services allow you to specify a portfolio of shares and obtain a valuation in one operation. They also allow you to search for companies by name and by category. They carry news archives which are very useful when investigating a target company.

Real-Time Prices

If you want to trade on a daily basis, in shares, options, or futures, you need to know the prices of these instruments as they change. A real time data feed is not the same as obtaining a quotation on a selected company from an internet site. For real time trading you need to have each price change as it occurs and to be able to store these and view them on a chart. The internet is not really suitable for this kind of data transmission, and real time data feeds usually use radio, tv, or satellite broadcasting channels.

You can obtain a real-time data feed from a number of suppliers, but they are relatively expensive. There is a basic charge for the software that runs on your computer, for the hardware that converts the signal to a computer feed and for the overall service. There are also fees that must be paid to the exchanges whose prices you opt to receive. For a reasonable cover, you will be paying a minimum of about £100 per month, so you should be sure you can make good profits before attempting to get involved with day trading.

The main providers in the UK are:

Market Eye: This system uses the BBC-2 teletext channel to broadcast its data. The data is received and decoded by a board which plugs into the mother-board of your PC computer. It takes its video feed from a BBC-2 TV antenna.

UpData-Prestel: They also use television broadcast channels to send their data. The receiver and decoder are in an external box that connects to the serial socket of your computer. This box takes its video feed from a BBC-2 antenna.

Tenfore Systems: They use a satellite to broadcast data for which you need a satellite dish. They supply a box of electronics to receive the video signal and convert it to a computer feed. The datadecoding is done by a board which plugs into the mother-board of your PC computer.

SBC Signal: This company also uses a satellite channel, and you need a satellite dish and a satellite receiver. They supply a box of electronics that does the decoding, and connects into the serial socket of your computer.

All of the above data feed companies supply software which runs on a PC. The format of the data display is different in each case, but generally, you can view price changes of several instruments simultaneously, and store many more. All have real-time charting facilities, that is, the data can be displayed as a graph of price against time, which adds new points as prices change. Thus you can see the short term price history of the instrument you are tracking.

This kind of real time data feed is essential if you are speculating. However, you need to watch it fairly consistently in order to take advantage of the sudden swings in price that make speculation so exciting. This activity is more like a full time job than amateur investing, and unless you can afford the time and the margin, it is not worthwhile paying for such complete and comprehensive data.

Chapter Eight

Misfortunes, Mistakes, and Deliberate Fraud: What to do when things go wrong

There are two main reasons why a company's share price may fall. The most common one is that the market, as a whole, has also fallen. More rarely, it is due to a perceived failure in the company's performance. Mistakes by management have already been covered in previous chapters and in the next chapter we shall discuss the causes of general market downturns.

However, whatever the cause of a price fall, we still have to decide what to do about it. To the investor who holds the shares, it may seem frivolous to enquire why the price has plunged, his immediate concern is to either sell the stock or stick with it. As usual, this decision is not easy to take, and even though first instincts may demand immediate action, it is necessary to stay calm, and examine the circumstances before deciding what action to take.

Downturns, Corrections, and Crashes

The financial press have many names that describe situations in which market prices are falling. A small, quick, dip may be attributed to 'profit taking'. A larger drop is called a 'technical correction' if it is brief, or a 'downturn' if it persists for any length of time. If the fall continues for a period of many months, then it is said to be a 'bear market'. A very large, sudden, fall is called a 'crash', and since these are rare events, like vintage wine, they are labelled according to their year. Thus, we have the crash of '29, and those of '73 and '87. In the day-to-day fluctuation of market prices, it is impossible to tell if profit taking will lead to a technical correction, if a correction will lengthen into a downturn and perhaps a bear market. It is unlikely, but not impossible, that it will avalanche into a full scale crash.

After some acquaintance with the financial press, it gradually becomes clear to the investor that the names given to the various forms of price fluctuation are simply that - names - they are not explanations. Market prices are driven by the actions of many buyers and sellers, all with individual motivations. There are simply too many of them to act in co-ordination. Although some large investors can force large price changes, no one can make the price go either up or down for very long. Since there is no way of predicting the actions of the market participants, the price level will fluctuate in an unpredictable way.

In addition, economic conditions are also varying, more or less randomly, so both the long and short term market trends are impossible to predict consistently.

However, there is one feature of market behaviour that is predictable, and that is over-reaction. Although the event which precipitates a drop is unpredictable, the drop itself is usually overdone, and likewise, when something happens to cause a rise, the price will overshoot. Given this phenomenon, it is wise not to react immediately when prices fall, because it is highly likely that they will recover, at least a little, after their initial plunge. This gives the wise investor a breathing space, a short period of grace in which to make his 'sell or stick' decision.

In this chapter we shall consider what to do when prices fall, either because of adverse economic conditions or disappointing company performance. However, it is first necessary to examine the nature of assets and why their prices are so volatile.

The Nature of Assets

Assets are bought and sold on markets, thus their price fluctuates according to supply and demand. However, there is one important difference between asset markets and markets for goods and services. When the demand for some consumer item increases, the companies that make it can increase production and so supply more items to the market. Similarly, when a particular service is in greater demand, more people will be drawn into that occupation. However, though an increase in demand for assets raises their price, it does not increase the amount of such assets in existence. This is one reason why asset prices swing much more widely than prices of goods and services.

The creation of assets, (capital formation) takes place mainly through growth within existing companies, and this process is largely independent of share prices. Thus, while the share price of a company which is growing may increase, the converse is not true - an increase in the share price of a company will not cause it to grow. On the other hand, when asset prices are low, capital formation does not stop or even decrease for this reason.

Companies will invest their profits in new plant only if they think that they can make more profits by doing so. This depends largely on the price at which it can sell its goods and services. Thus, capital formation responds to the price levels in the market for goods and services, not that of assets.

The market for assets is a second hand market which facilitates the transfer of assets but plays no significant part in their creation. Thus, new money coming into the market drives up prices without increasing supply. Instead of new assets appearing in the market, the owners of existing assets have to be persuaded to sell them by an increase in price. Furthermore, the money paid to the original owners is not generally spent outside the market, but remains available to buy other assets. Cash rich investment funds have only two homes for their money. In the short term they may keep their money in a bank - in the long term they must put it into assets.

Of course, when share prices are high, private organisations are tempted to convert themselves into public companies and 'float' themselves on the market.

However, these are not new assets, they are existing assets changing the market on which they are traded. The money paid for these companies when they float goes largely to the investment funds which originally backed them, so again, the cash stays in the market to chase up the price of other assets.

It is also true that companies in need of cash can sell new shares into the market, or even issue bonds, as an alternative to borrowing from banks. This takes money out of the asset markets but it does not create new assets unless the company uses the money to buy new equipment. Unfortunately, this is a rare practice in the UK, and when companies do obtain cash in this way, it is usually to pay off bank debt or other creditors. In neither the short term nor the long term does this lead to an increase in actual assets.

By far the biggest issuer of bonds is government, both local and central. However, money raised by the sale of such bonds is usually spent on balancing budgets and not on new capital formation schemes. Nevertheless, these bond issues do take money out of the asset market. In practice, they are one of the factors which limit the rise of asset prices. It is when share prices are very high and yields very low, that new bond issues usually make their appearance.

Speculation

On any normal day on the asset markets, there will be a large number of people buying and selling assets, and for a variety of reasons. As well as the pension funds, investment trusts, the steady savers and wise investors, there will be others with more urgent motivation - the speculators. Since their buying and selling is short term, it is their activity that causes most of the shorter term variations in prices.

141

The effects of speculation are magnified by two practices which may seem unfair to the private investor. The first is the custom of banks lending money to speculators to buy shares. The second is the custom of allowing speculators to sell shares they do not own. Thus when asset markets are trending upwards, speculators buy shares on 'margin'. That is, the shares act as collateral for the loan, rather like a mortgage. This process is self-reinforcing, as the markets rise, so the value of the collateral rises, and so more money can be borrowed to buy more shares. When markets are trending down, speculators are allowed to sell shares they do not own, in the expectation that after a short time they will be able to buy them back at a lower price.

It is often claimed that speculation is beneficial in that it makes the market more 'liquid'. It is true, speculators do create liquidity, but they create it when it is already sufficient, i.e., when prices are rising. When liquidity is most needed - when prices are falling - they act to destroy it. By selling shares they do not own they take cash from the market which would have gone to sellers who actually own shares. Over all, in as much as speculators make profits, they take money out of the markets, which is a net reduction in liquidity. The truth is that successful speculation relies on price swings, and it increases rather than decreases them.

The swings in the level of asset prices are not predictable in any absolute sense. For the reasons given above, the variations from high to low over a particular period are far greater than price changes in the markets for goods and services. However, speculators do not significantly influence long term price movements.

The surest way for the private investor to profit is by 'knowing' that a certain company has better than average chances of growing its earnings. Even if the market price falls in the short term, the long term result of earnings growth must be a higher share price. This is the superior return we are looking for, but to obtain it we must resist the temptation to follow fashions, jump on bandwagons, or panic when prices fall.

Asset Price Inflation: Bubbles

A 'Bubble' is the name given to extreme, temporary, asset price inflation. The term originated in the primitive stock markets of early eighteenth century London. The most famous Bubble of all was the 'South Sea Bubble' which ruined many investors and brought imprisonment to the company managers and several members of the British Parliament. The South Sea Company was set up in the early 1700s to trade with the new colonies in South America, and was modelled on the hugely successful East India Company.

Unfortunately for the investors, South America was at that time under the total control of Spain. However, they were not discouraged by this, nor by the fact that only one British ship per year was permitted to trade there, and that the Spanish king demanded 25% of the profits. South Sea Company stock was traded in 'Exchange Alley' - the part of London used by 'stock jobbers' to buy and sell shares.

It was a time of prosperity and people were beginning to look for ways of investing their savings, rather than hoarding them as silver and gold coin. The South Sea Company was only one of many companies at that time that were selling stock with virtually no asset backing. Its fame lies in the fact that it did it more successfully, and with more disastrous consequences, than any of the others.

In the year 1720, the South Sea Company began to negotiate with parliament to take over the British National Debt. This relationship with government greatly increased the prestige of the stock. Throughout the summer of that year, the stock gradually rose from 100 to 1000, with new stock being issued without restraint. There was scarce enough income to pay dividends on the existing stock and these new issues were effectively worthless.

When the price crashed it did so within a few days, and angry investors crowded the streets. Riots threatened the capital and parliament ordered an enquiry. Not surprisingly, it was found that the managers were guilty of fraud. The market may have been primitive, but the techniques that were used to manipulate prices have hardly been improved upon in three hundred years. The managers had used fictitious names on certificates, bribed members of parliament with gifts of stock, but most of all, they had been very active in manufacturing rumours favourable to the share price. Most damming in the eyes of the public was that the managers had sold out shortly before the crash, and to many this proved that they had actually caused the crash.

In retrospect, it is clear that the conditions in the early 1700s were conducive to inflation bubbles. Investors were relatively unsophisticated, and there was a general lack of understanding about financial assets. However, the main factor was the availability of savings to be invested, largely because the hoarding of coin had become unfashionable. With so much hot money chasing new assets, the creation of bogus assets can almost be regarded as natural phenomena. The public were conditioned by the example of the East India Company to believe that overseas trade was a source of great wealth. It was this that favoured the South Sea Company over the other investment opportunities of the time.

Assets are worth what someone is willing to pay. When an asset has a yield, then it can be compared with other assets that have yields, and some relative value established on which to base a sensible price. When an asset has no current yield, then its value is based on its future yield, which can only be estimated, guessed at, or hoped for. The limit to this 'hope' value depends only on the power of human imagination fuelled by human greed, and urged on by human persuasion.

Asset prices can rise, therefore, not because there is an increase in the yield of the asset, but because people think there could be, or might be, or simply hope that there will be. In the human heart, hope springs eternal, and in the hearts of investors, this hope frequently translates into a willingness to pay high prices for shares which have no earnings.

Given a share price that is rising on hope, an even worse situation may then ensue. The increase in price itself may become the return that speculators are looking for. When this happens there is no limit to the price rise as investors go for quick profits. A bubble is precisely this kind of situation and the name is very apt. It suggests something rising in the air, getting larger and larger, full of iridescent colour that attracts the eye and holds the attention.

The name is accurate, too, in that every bubble is destined to burst and disappear. Each investor knows this, but thinks that the others do not. They know they are investing, not for any long term gain, but for a quick profit. They imagine that they will be able to sell out before the collapse. It is like getting on a train that is heading for the edge of a cliff, going faster and faster. You plan to get out just as soon as the cliff top comes into sight, but the reality is that the train will not be stopping - the driver and his friends got out at the last stop.

The cause of inflationary bubbles is grounded in human nature. Fortunately, when investors go mad, they do so for only a short period and bubbles are short lived phenomena.

However, there are other forces at work in our economic system, which are part of the system itself. These produce longer lasting swings in the price level of asset markets that even the wisest investor cannot avoid. These longer term swings are a consequence of the business cycle, and this is discussed in the next chapter.

Getting caught up in a bubble might qualify as a misfortune, especially if those involved did not really intend the scheme to get out of hand so dramatically. It may be that a wise investor can easily avoid these situations. However, dishonest men are always on the look out for ways and means of taking other people's money, and the financial markets are not immune. The most frequent kind of financial fraud is known as a ponzi scheme, and we will now look at how this works.

Ponzi Schemes

Charles Ponzi was an Italian immigrant to the USA, living in Boston. In 1919 he set up 'The Securities Exchange Company', purporting to deal in postage coupons, from which Ponzi claimed to be making 400% profit. He offered to let others share in these fabulous profits by issuing loan notes on which he promised to pay 50% profit in 90 days. The scheme ran for several months throughout the summer of 1920 during which he defrauded 10,000 investors of $9,500,000. At today's values, this is equivalent to approximately $500 million.

The 'postage coupons', which were supposed to provide the profits, derived from prepaid postage arrangements with countries outside the USA. Because the first world war had disrupted currency exchange rates, these coupons could now be bought at different prices in different countries.

Theoretically, Ponzi really could make 400% profit by buying 25 cent coupons for the equivalent of 5 cents each in Spain. However, to make it worthwhile he would have had to buy millions of such coupons, and he would also have had to find someone willing to buy them. Ponzi refused to say how he was selling the coupons, claiming that this was a legitimate business secret.

The authorities, sensing that something was wrong, directed their initial investigations at the coupons business. They claimed that Ponzi could not purchase and re-sell sufficient coupons to utilise the massive amounts of money his fund was taking in. Of course, that was not a problem for Ponzi because he wasn't buying coupons at all. There were no profits - he was paying the interest on earlier loan notes with the new loans coming in.

This kind of scam can only go on so long as the fund is growing. At first, the public is sceptical, but when it is seen that the large dividends are being paid, more and more people subscribe to the scheme. This process will continue until all the available 'hot money' has been sucked into the fund.

Then, as soon as the flow stops, the manager stops paying the dividend and the scheme collapses.

In Ponzi's schemes, only the managers of his bank, the Hanover Trust, realised what he was doing. The bank had so much money coming into its accounts that the managers were reluctant to do anything that might stop the flow. Ponzi ensured their continued silence by buying a 38% share in the bank. The scheme carried on for several months, until, eventually, Ponzi failed to pay the interest, and the fund collapsed. Within two days, so did the bank. There was a trial and Ponzi was convicted of fraud and sent to prison.

This incident was really an old trick that had been played before and has been played since. Nevertheless, Ponzi played it better and bigger than anyone else, and his name is now associated with this type of fraud. However, Ponzi's story wasn't entirely typical for deceptions of this kind. The originators of such schemes usually disappear as soon as the fund has reached its maximum value, and of course, most of the money disappears with them.

However, Ponzi did not run off with the money. In fact, he showed all the signs of settling into the Boston area, buying a large house from his gains. Why he did not take the money and run is a mystery, He had previously been imprisoned for operating an illegal immigrant racket, so he had the contacts necessary to make an effective getaway. Perhaps, like his bank managers, he was hypnotised by the flood of money. Perhaps he enjoyed the life style of the successful businessman that he appeared to be, and didn't realise that the end would come so soon, or so suddenly.

Ponzi schemes are not always so obviously fraudulent as the eponymous original. The investment story is often very plausible, gold mines in Siberia, oil fields in Persia, diamonds from South Africa, or any other thing that will capture investors' imagination. In these frauds, the investment idea is always different, but the offer of high returns is always the same.

147

Some schemes only reveal themselves to be fraudulent after several years, and even then, failure may appear as cruel misfortune rather than criminal intent. In some cases it is impossible to judge, even with hindsight, if the managers originally intended to defraud the investors. It may be that the managers began with good intentions, and only turned criminal when the investments started to fail. For example, a fund which offered a return of 15% per annum might just be able to achieve that. If it couldn't, then the managers, faced with personal financial ruin, might then decide to quit while they are ahead.

Since this book is about investing in companies directly rather than in funds, this discussion might seem to be unnecessary. However, Ponzi schemes are not confined to investment funds. Many company frauds are essentially Ponzi Schemes, albeit accidental ones. Company managers sometimes get caught up in a cycle of money raising, firmly believing that it will all come right in the end. At least, that is what they say when the company finally goes bust. These companies are characterised by a constant need for new investment, sometimes for new equipment, sometimes in order to develop a product which will, they claim, bring in enormous profits. Almost always, at the outset, the managers of these companies believe their own optimistic prospectus.

Some interesting case histories are to be found in the old heavy industries which were dependent on large amounts of capital equipment much in need of modernisation. A typical company would still be paying dividends, but instead of buying new equipment out of earnings, it would ask the shareholders for more cash on the basis that re-equipping would be a one-off exercise.

A company can raise cash by making a 'rights issue' of new shares. Each existing shareholder has the right to buy new shares, and is invited to do so. However, since there will soon be more shares in issue, the dividends will almost certainly fall. Consequently, the shareholders are being asked to pay more for less. The dividends that are paid come from income that should have been used to buy new equipment. The assets are not being depreciated at the proper rate so the shareholders are really being paid out of their own capital.

This exercise is often called a 'recapitalisation'. If it occurs just once then it can be a valid way for a company to get out of a difficult situation. However, recapitalisations seem to be habit forming, and when they occur year after year, they are effectively Ponzi schemes, which eventually must come to their usual, disastrous end.

Sell or Stick

Deliberate or 'accidental' fraud is quite rare. When the shareholder finds that his investment is falling in value, it is usually for other reasons. The most common is that asset prices, in general, are falling. The reasons for this are given in the next chapter, and unfortunately, there is not much that can be done by way of selling and reinvesting. However, a wise investor keeps track of events, watching the price of his shares rise and fall.

The normal fluctuations of market prices will ensure that whatever happens, the prices will not stay constant. However, an investor need only contemplate taking action when his shares have fallen from their peak by a significant amount. Warren Buffet advises investors to be prepared to see their investments fall by as much as 50% before being stirred into action. However, it is unlikely that a private investor will have such strong confidence in his investments to be able to watch calmly as they halve in price. So we shall use a more modest criterion. Given the volatility of equity markets, 10% seems a reasonable figure to use and it is easy to calculate. Fluctuations within this limit can be attributed to randomness.

Thus, when a company's share price falls by 10% or more from its peak, we shall deem it necessary to find out what caused the fall, and decide what, if anything, to do about it. Variations within this limit we shall attribute to Mr Market's moodiness. Assuming, then that a price fall has exceeded this limit, and to find out why, the first thing we do is round up the usual suspects:

i) the company itself;
ii) the economic sector;
iii) the national economy; and
iv) the world economy.

Comparing the fall in the share price to the relevant market indices can identify the guilty party. If the company's sector is healthy then the company itself is to blame. If the sector is down and the national economy is not, then clearly, something is wrong in the sector. If both the sector and the country are down and the world is still doing well, then the national economy needs to be looked at. If the world economy is down, then at least we have the satisfaction of knowing that everyone else is suffering too.

When the share price fall is due to company performance, then the investor may have made a bad decision. He bought the shares in the expectation of earnings growth, and if that growth has not materialised in the way predicted, then he must consider selling. Once he is satisfied that the situation is irretrievable, then at the first sign of a rally in the share price he should sell. It is easy to take profits, but very painful to take losses, and courage is needed to admit that a mistake has been made. The sooner the mistake is recognised the sooner you will have the chance to do better. As the saying has it, 'take your losses on the chin'.

Riding out the Storm

If your shares fall due to a general decline in asset markets, then it is necessary to estimate the duration of the downturn. Unfortunately, there is no really effective way to do this. The only rule that can be used is that the more widespread the downturn, the longer it will take for it to work through. However, if there is a single specific reason for the fall, then a reversal of that condition can often reverse the fall quite quickly. A recent example is the Gulf war - Operation Desert Storm. This caused a general fall in world market prices because of the danger that the USA might suffer a military setback. The successful result of the war brought the world markets back to their previous levels. The whole process took less than a year to work through.

Clearly it would have been wrong to sell out at the height of the Gulf war, when prices were low. In fact, this was a good time to be thinking of buying. The Rothschild family have a motto that has served them well for hundreds of years. 'Buy when the enemy is at the gates, sell when the victory trumpet sounds'. Using this rule would have enabled you to buy good shares during the Gulf war, and also in the first and second world wars. But keeping your savings in cash waiting for world war III is not a wise thing to do.

On a long term view, the markets always come back from a downturn, so a sensible decision would be to stick, and this is what Warren Buffet recommends. However, our portfolio has a finite lifetime, and we may not have time to wait for prices to recover, as they surely will. The duration of a downturn in asset prices is dependent on its cause. The discussion in the next chapter will give some insight into the reasons for long term asset price swings, and this can be used to help make a sensible 'sell or stick' decision. If you are within five years of retiring then the sell or stick decision is exceptionally difficult. One compensating factor in favour of a sell decision is that a fall in asset prices usually causes a rise in dividends on fixed interest instruments. Switching to an income portfolio and locking into high income might then be a wise move.

However, for investors who already have an income portfolio, the decision must almost always be to 'stick'. Since most of the investments should be in fixed interest instruments, a crash in asset prices would only affect the asset valuation of the portfolio. The income would be largely unaltered, and since this is the objective of the portfolio, it would be unwise to sell it. If we sell out and put the money in a bank account, it would not bring in much more in interest, and this income would fall as soon as bank interest rates began to fall. So the best advice must be to stick with the portfolio. The exception to this is for preference shares. If the company whose shares you hold is in financial difficulty, then it may decide to miss out the dividends, which it is legally entitled to do. In this case, a sell or stick decision can be made by the usual process for evaluating a company's business.

Chapter Nine

Money, Banks and the Business Cycle.

Banks

A bank is the place where we keep our money, if we have some, and where we can borrow more if we don't have enough. Money is the reason for the existence of banking, and before we can attempt to understand how banks work we need first to take a good look at the nature of money itself.

The nature of money

We are all very familiar with money. It is what we work for, what we spend, and what we save. We obtain money in return for our labour and skill, then we exchange it for the goods and services we need. This means we do not have to barter the things we have for the things we want. Money allows earning and spending to be two separate transactions, and without it modern life would be impossible.

When we have earned money there is not usually much delay before we spend it, a few days or weeks, maybe months. Earning and spending are overlapping processes. To keep it running smoothly we keep a small stock of money from which we can buy the things we need on a day-to-day basis, and which is topped up, weekly or monthly by our earnings. This can be a current account with a bank, a wallet or purse in which we can keep notes and coins, or more usually, both.

Saving money is different. We earn money with a view to accumulating it, usually in a bank account, so that we can build up a fund of money to spend at some date in the future. We may be saving to buy an expensive item, or we may just want to have a reserve of money available for financial emergencies. Alternatively, we can use a savings account as a temporary home for money before investing it in a pension fund.

The time period between earning money and spending it, is one of the confusing things about money. It seems unfair that in this interval of time, the value of our money can change, almost always in a downward direction. This is the reason why investment is a better way of storing value than a bank account. Even though banks are willing to pay interest on the money we save, inflation will increase the price of the things we eventually wish to buy. This loss of purchasing power is such that sometimes money loses value at a greater rate than interest can increase it.

In our day-to-day financial dealings we take for granted that money exists in two distinct forms. There is the cash we have in our wallets and purses, and there is the money we keep in our bank accounts. Since, in a modern economy we can exchange one for the other with such ease, we tend not to think of them as being different. However, the difference between cash and account money, between the tangible and the abstract, is the very essence of banking. Bank profits depend almost entirely on loans made via accounts and very little on cash advanced across the counter.

In discussing these two different kinds of money, we will refer to the money we hold in the form of notes and coins, as 'cash' or 'tangible' money. The money that we have in a bank will be called 'account' money or 'abstract' money.

Money isn't what it used to be. In the last 100 years, we have moved from a system based on gold to a system based on trust. We no longer carry a bag of gold and silver coins, or hoard them in a strong box under the bed. The coins and bank notes which we keep for occasional expenses, have no intrinsic value, they are simply tokens. The rest of our money we keep in the form of bank accounts, which are just numbers in ledgers.

In order to understand how money became what it is today, we need to look at the development of money and how it evolved into the thing we are all so familiar with.

The Evolution of Money

It is well known that, in ancient times, trade was carried out by barter. Essentially, if I grew corn, and you kept cattle, then we would exchange corn for cows at an agreed rate of so many bags of corn for one cow. This is not a very convenient way of trading. Even if I did want a whole cow, you might not want the large amount of corn you would receive in exchange for it. Instead, you might want some corn and some wool from a third person who kept sheep. Of course, I might want some wool too, and so we would now have a three-way trade. If we include all the other things which others are producing and which we might want, in small or large quantities according to our individual needs, then trading by direct barter is impossible.

According to historians, the first people to use coined money were the Lydians, who prospered in the Mediterranean about three thousand years ago. A coin is simply a very small metal ingot of standard weight and purity guaranteed by the king whose head is stamped on it. The most convenient metals for this purpose are gold, silver, and to a lesser extent, copper. They are precious enough to be valuable in small amounts, soft enough to be stamped out by hand, yet durable enough to survive long usage. The only other metals used in the ancient world for this purpose were electrum, an alloy of gold and silver, and bronze an alloy of copper and tin.

Using precious metal as money is simply an elaborate form of barter since the metal itself is useful and therefore valuable for its own sake. This kind of money is called 'commodity' money because the metal itself is a valued commodity in the economic system in which it is used. In the course of civilisation, other objects and substances have been used in this way. Cowry shells were used all over the pacific for thousands of years, right up to world war two. Tobacco served this purpose in the early American colonies. More recently, in the late 1940's, cigarettes were used as a medium of exchange in occupied Germany.

In Anglo-Saxon times, the currency in England was the silver penny. This was standardised at 240 silver pennies minted (or 'struck') from one pound weight of silver. The silver was defined as 92.5% pure, which later came to be known as Sterling silver. As the years passed, the weight of the penny was reduced, and by the year 1600, a pound of silver was being minted into 480 pennies. However, the number of pennies in the monetary pound remained at 240. Thus the pound Sterling of money and the pound weight of silver were no longer the same. Attempts to degrade the quality of the coins were not so successful. When silver coins went out of use in 1946, the sixpenny piece was about the same size as the Anglo-Saxon penny. However, the standard of purity was the same as that set by the Anglo-Saxons over 1000 years before.

Special problems arise if both gold and silver coins circulate together in the same economic system. When the coins are originally minted, their relative value and weight are in the same ratio. However, as the supply conditions of the two metals change over time, one or other will become more valuable as metal in terms of the other as coin.

For example, when Isaac Newton was master of the royal mint in 1719, he fixed the value of the golden guinea at 21 shillings, equivalent to £1.05.

This proved slightly too high, and the silver coinage was now worth more than its face value compared to gold. So that 21 silver shillings melted down and sold as bullion would be worth more than one guinea. In consequence, silver began to disappear from circulation. To solve this problem, in 1819 the Bank of England made the silver coins very much smaller so that their value as metal was much less than their face value. Since that date, even silver coins have been, in effect, token money.

In 1816, the inconvenient 21 shilling guinea was replaced by the £1 sovereign coin, which continued to circulate in Britain until 1914. In many remote parts of the world, the sovereign is still used as money. It is the gold coin that people still accept with confidence. The equivalent silver coin still used as money is the Austrian Dollar (Thaler) which originated in the reign of Empress Maria Theresa. This coin is still minted bearing her head and the date 1751. Likewise sovereigns are still produced by the royal mint, but with the head of the reigning monarch and the true year of issue.

The metallic money we use in Britain today is token money even though the coins do have some small, intrinsic value. The metals are generally alloys of nickel and copper. This money is called 'token' money since the coins are just convenient tokens and might as well be made of plastic or any other cheap and durable substance. Bank notes are a special kind of token money in which the intrinsic value of the material and production costs are reduced to a minimum. The temptation to forgery, therefore, is increased to a maximum. As technology progresses, the paper of bank notes is being augmented by plastic, and special devices, such as metal strips, water marks, and holograms, are being used to discourage forgers.

Bank notes came into use in Britain in the 1630's. In the early days of banking, when you took your metal money to a bank, the banker gave you a receipt indicating the amount of cash you had deposited. When you wanted to recover your money, you simply took this receipt back to the bank and asked them to 'redeem' it with cash. It didn't take long for businessmen to realise that these receipts could be used as a form of money. Instead of going to the bank with your receipt you simply gave it to your creditor. He could then either go to the bank and redeem it for cash, or pass the note on to his creditors. The banks encouraged the practice of note circulation by issuing receipts in convenient denominations, and promising to pay the 'bearer' rather than the original depositor. The standard bank note is simply a note from the bank promising to pay the bearer a certain sum of money. Originally, the bank note promised to pay in gold or silver coin. However, modern bank notes simply promise to exchange the note for another note, or token coins of the same face value.

Modern bank notes have a distinction which is denied to all other kinds of money. They are legal tender for the payment of debts and they are 'negotiable'. This idea is very important for a modern economy. It means that anyone who accepts a negotiable note obtains undisputed right to it, even if it has been stolen. Money must have this property, otherwise creditors could claim back money already spent by defaulting borrowers. If you rob a bank and use the money to buy a car, the bank cannot ask the motor company to return 'their' money. Whereas, if the bank manager's car is stolen, it remains his property, and he can claim it back.

Gold and silver were used as a basis for money for thousands of years, up to 1914 in Britain, and 1971 in the USA. However, the circulation of precious metal coins as money could not be sustained because there just wasn't enough of these metals to cover the ever increasing economic activity. Of course, new supplies of gold and silver were constantly being found, but the amount of this supply was not related to the needs of the economy. New supplies of precious metals depend on the accidental discovery of mineable ores, whereas the need for money depends on the amount of economic activity which a community can sustain without serious inflation.

In a modern industrialised state, almost all the money used in commerce and private life is abstract money in the form of bank accounts. It exists only on paper and in computer memory, as the bank's records. For day-to-day transactions in shops and offices, we use tangible money which is now token coins and bank notes. We no longer use a gold or silver standard to sustain the value of our currency, and there are no gold or silver coins in circulation whose intrinsic value is equal to their face value

Abstract money in the form of accounts is created by the commercial banks. If we wish to convert this to tangible money, the banks are happy for us to withdraw it in the form of notes and coins. This token money is supplied to the commercial banks by the central bank, which controls its manufacture and distribution. The commercial banks have accounts with the central bank and they can withdraw coins and notes in exactly the same way as their own customers do.

In the days of gold, if a large number of people decided to take their money as cash, there would be a 'run on the bank' and the bank might fail. Now, if people wanted to keep their money as cash, the central bank would simply manufacture enough of it to satisfy the demand.

Given that both abstract and tangible money are thus so easy to create, the potential for over-creation would seem to be very great, and indeed it is. Since Britain went off the gold standard in 1914, the real value of the pound has declined by a factor of about 54 up to 1994. That is an average decline of 5% per year for 80 years. In contrast, while on a precious metal standard during the previous 800 years, the pound declined by an average of 0.4% per year.

It is now the duty of the Bank of England, in its role as the central bank, to control inflation. To do this, the level of price inflation is continuously monitored, and the central bank exerts influence on the commercial banks to moderate the rate at which they create abstract money in the form of bank loans and overdrafts.

Our present banking system works well though not perfectly. It is the end result of a long and painful process of evolution during which banks and bankers only gradually came under any centralised control. In fact, the early days of banking were part of the growth of free enterprise, and banks were just as likely to fail as any other company. It is appropriate to look at this development.

Banks and Money Supply

The story of banking is that of the struggle to overcome the shortage of gold and silver which are the metals from which money is traditionally made.

At first, the banks simply lent their own money, acting effectively as money-lenders. Later they began to lend the money they were supposed to be keeping safe for others. Initially bank loans consisted of gold and silver coin so that, obviously, banks could not lend more than they had. Banks were essentially recycling cash from those who had more than they needed to those who needed more than they had.

Then the banks discovered that they could reduce the need to lend out metallic money if customers with the same bank were encouraged to pay their debts to each other by cheque. Payment is then effected by transferring money between accounts within the banking system, so that gold and silver coins do not leave the bank. In this case, the money used is abstract since the bank transfers an obligation from one customer to another.

Once bank accounts became common, the banks found it convenient to make loans by allowing account holders to run up overdrafts. Here the bank is creating abstract money in the form of debit accounts. Again, no metallic money is required in this process, and the bank simply adjusts its records. Of course, if the borrower takes cash from his overdrawn account then metallic money is involved, and the bank must allow for this possibility.

However, it soon became clear to the bankers that they could lend more money than they had. They discovered that, in practice, the total amount of debit account loans could easily exceed the value of their gold and silver reserves. So long as most account holders were happy to keep their money in the bank, no one would know that the loans were not covered by gold and silver coins.

Finally, banks found they could issue bank notes in place of gold and silver coins. That is, they could substitute token money for commodity money. Originally, bank notes were simply a proxy for the gold and silver held in their vaults. However, bankers soon found they could issue notes above and beyond the value of their gold and silver reserves. This was a second method by which a bank could lend more money that it had. Again, so long as most of their note holders were happy to hold their money as notes, no one would know that they were not entirely covered by gold and silver coins.

These techniques may be summarised as follows:
1. the advancing of loans from deposits, that is the recycling of savings;
2. the use of cheques drawn on bank accounts;
3. the advancing of loans based on debit bank accounts; and
4. the issue of bank notes (and token coins) not covered by gold or silver.

For thousands of years, commercial transactions were carried out using money based on gold and silver. Even when banks began to create abstract money in the form of bank accounts, the assumption was that only gold and silver coins were 'real' money. Bank notes in those days promised to pay 'on demand' the face value of the note in gold or silver coin.

While most people were content to use token money or hold their money in abstract form in a bank account, they always felt that money was backed, ultimately by gold and silver. In times of financial crisis, cautious people often withdrew money from their accounts as coin, and presented bank notes for redemption in cash. However, so long as a bank had sufficient gold and silver reserves to meet this 'run on the bank' the public would be reassured.

Token money and bank accounts are so convenient that people really prefer them to the alternative of carrying bags of gold and silver coins. The convenience of paying by cheque makes it unlikely that people would ever want to return to cash transactions for large payments. The essential requirement of a monetary system is not so much that the money should itself be precious, but that it can always be used to buy the things we need, and that its value in terms of these things should not fall too rapidly as time passes.

In the last 100 years, banking has progressed from lending money based on gold and silver, to creating money based only on trust. A modern bank has no gold and silver in its vaults, just bank notes, bonds, share certificates, and other 'paper assets'. How this change came about and how modern banks work, is the subject of the next section.

Development of Banking Practice

Historically, banking developed from the ancient practice of money lending. There were banks of this kind in ancient Athens and throughout the Roman Empire. To keep the story short we shall look only at the development of banking in Britain and the United States of America, which, in their own evolution, rediscovered the practices of the ancient world and invented some new ones of their own.

About the time that the first settlers in the American colonies were building their log cabins, the goldsmiths of London began to provide a primitive banking service. At first, this was money lending and the provision of safe keeping for other people's gold and silver. The money they lent was originally their own, but as deposits built up in their strong rooms, they yielded to the temptation to lend out their customers' money as well. It is unclear to what extent their customers were aware of this practice. The fact that the goldsmiths were now able to offer interest on money deposited with them instead of charging a storage fee, suggests that their depositors knew of the general practice if not the details. Whatever the morality of the situation, the effects were beneficial. This was the first stage of banking - the recycling of money from the conservative rich to the enterprising poor.

The modern banking practices of taking deposits, cashing cheques, issuing bank notes, and making loans, all appeared in London during the early part of the 1600's. However, bankers were still tentative in making loans. They knew that they could lend their customers' money with relative safety. However, they were unsure about how much 'extra' money they could lend above and beyond the amount of precious metal they held in their vaults. By 1700, the use of bank accounts and payment by cheque had become accepted as an essential part of commercial life in London. It was acknowledged that banks could make loans simply by opening accounts for borrowers and allowing them to overdraw. Therefore, the granting of a loan did not result in a corresponding decrease in the amount of gold and silver in the bank's vaults. A safe ratio of loans to cash was found to be about ten to one. That is, from a cash base of, say, £1 million, the bank can lend £10 million.

These 'debit accounts' were more or less subject to the same conditions as accounts in credit, and only a few of the cheques drawn on either accounts were presented for cash payment.

In effect, the banks were creating abstract money in the form of debit accounts. So long as this money was used only for transactions between account holders, there was no need to have gold and silver coins to support it.

The money supplied by these means was used to finance Britain's growing commercial activities, in particular, the planting of colonies in various parts of the world. In the 1690's, the wars of William the third required so much money that his government began to look for ways of acquiring it without the disagreeable expedient of raising taxes.

This resulted in the formation of the Bank of England, a bank specially chartered to raise loans for the government and to act as its banker. In 1694, the bank opened its books with a loan of £1.2 million to the government and the public rushed to subscribe.

The main condition of the loan was that the bank was allowed to issue the same amount of money in bank notes. Thus, the government got the loan, the subscribers got fair interest guaranteed by the government, and the bank got the benefit of the note issue together with the prestige of running the government's financial affairs. Thus began the Bank of England - at first just another bank, and thus began the British national debt - at first just another short term loan.

In its American colonies, Britain had an effective monopoly of banking. When paper money appeared about 1660, it was issued, not by banks, but by state governments. In the face of a chronic shortage of money to finance expanding economic activities, several states took it upon themselves to make note issues. Since this avoided the immediate need to raise taxes they were quite popular. These notes were successful in varying degrees; the best were always limited issues for a specific purpose, the worst were unlimited issues which, after inflation, ended up worthless.

Meanwhile, the colonies began to set up their own banks provoking the British commercial interests to act against them. In 1741, parliament was persuaded to employ legislation designed to stop speculation, the 'bubble acts' applied to the colonies and banking was effectively suppressed.

Again, in 1751, the British parliament passed a law prohibiting note issues by state governments, bringing these promising experiments to an end. This prohibition on financial experimentation caused great resentment and encouraged the popular movement for independence.

It is at this point in history British and American political and financial institutions go their separate ways. When the American Continental Congress made its declaration of independence in 1777, it was faced not only with setting up a system of political government, but also in deciding how such government should be financed. The immediate problem in this respect was how to find money to pay for the war of independence.

The new government did not have the power to impose taxes, nor did it have a bank, and it was impossible to enforce customs duties at ports still in the control of the British. It was inevitable then that it should turn to the only expedient left, printing its own money. Thus, the revolutionary government's first revolutionary act was to issue notes, and this it did in vast quantities. These were the 'continentals' which at first circulated at face value, but as the war progressed, fell in exchange against precious metal money and finally, after the war was won, became worthless.

Despite its victory, the central government was still weak and in the new constitution, the issue of notes by both state and central government, was banned. However, in 1791 it established the Bank of the United States. This state bank immediately began to act as a central bank to the commercial banks that were being opened over the whole country. The Bank of the United States was not popular with business. It had only been charted for twenty years, and a movement developed to close it down. This succeeded in 1810. After this, banking in the United States was largely unregulated and the number of banks grew at a prodigious rate.

On the eastern seaboard, the banks were relatively large and conservative, similar to European banks. In the West, banking entered new and uncharted territory in both senses. The demand for credit in the form of bank notes stimulated growth in the number of banks. Each area had its own bank that failed or flourished with the local economy. For the growing and mobile population of the western states, bank notes became the preferred way of expanding the money supply.

Each bank could issue its own notes which most did in large quantities. Bank failures were frequent, but since the banks were small, the negative effects were easily swallowed up in the general benefit which a flood of cheap finance brings to a rapidly expanding economy. The notes from many banks were only acceptable at less than their face value. They were like the separate currencies in Europe; each had its own exchange rate against gold and silver. Thus, the United States had the advantages of centralised political control without the nuisance of a centrally controlled supply of money for its widely different economic areas.

Meanwhile, back in Britain, the tendency in banking was increasingly towards centralisation. The Bank of England was a huge success. The government, having found that it could borrow cheaply via the bank, increased its borrowing. By 1748 the national debt was £71 million, by 1763 it was £128 million, by 1783 it was £238 million, and by the end of the Napoleonic wars in 1815 it was £820 million. There were severe problems in 1797, due to wars with both France and the new USA, and the bank had to suspend redemption of its notes in gold coin. In fact, so many notes were in issue that the price of gold bullion rose well above its official value against the pound. However, it fell again, and by 1821 the bank was once again able to exchange its notes for gold coin at the old rate.

After being forced to suspend redemption of its notes for 25 years, the Bank of England wanted to ensure that it did not happen again. Consequently, in 1844, the government prohibited the issue of bank notes in amounts greater than a bank's cash reserve. This meant that money could now only be created via debit accounts which favoured payment by cheque. Since cheque clearance requires banks to co-operate with each other, this became an important factor in the centralisation of British banking.

Britain, was a single state with a fairly homogeneous economy and a very centralised business community based on London. The Bank of England, gradually took over the issue of notes, and in 1844 began the custom of providing support for commercial banks in times of crisis. This was the final step to being the central bank, and despite the fact that it was a joint stock company, it acted in the interests of the government and the business community. The commercial banks became, effectively, branches of a state bank.

On the other hand, in the United State of America, the independently minded states had the advantage of competitive, independent banking. This was an optimum solution, the expanding states needed an expanding money supply, and the settled states needed stable money. The banking practices that evolved from 1810 to 1914 ensured that the country was settled, from coast to coast, in the shortest possible time.

While Britain adopted a gold standard, and encouraged gold coins to circulate along side bank notes, the banks in America issued mainly notes, each of which had an exchange rate against gold. The American system was much more flexible, permitting sound money in the east and more adaptable money in the West. It was not until the whole country became effectively one large economy, that the need for a central bank arose. The appropriate law was enacted in 1913 just in time for the first world war. The result was the Federal Reserve Bank.

Modern Banking

Without gold as backing, money is now intrinsically worthless, yet it works just as well as it ever it did. No one refuses to take bank notes even though banks no longer promise to redeem notes except with other notes. So long as token coins and notes are acceptable, they will circulate and perform all the functions of gold and silver money except that they cannot be hoarded with any real expectation that they will hold their value.

The supply of token money to the public is a service provided by the commercial banks for the convenience of their customers, and the banks obtain it from the central bank which controls its manufacture. Each commercial bank has an account with the central bank which must be kept in credit. Since this money can always be withdrawn as coins and notes it represents the bank's cash and it plays the same role as gold did in the old system.

The commercial banks still create money in the form of debit accounts, just as they did in the days of gold. This is the main supply of money to the economic system so that cheques and other methods of credit transfer are the main ways of paying debts. Cheques from one bank, presented for encashment at another bank, are cleared through a central clearing system. The net balances are settled through accounts at the central bank. If one bank lends more than its fair share, then it soon finds that some of the money it has created has 'leaked' to the other banks. Its account with the central bank soon begins to deplete. This effectively stops banks from competing too hard in making loans. So long as each bank keeps pace with the others in creating money, there is no risk of it losing all its reserves. This harmonising effect means that the banks can create as much money as they want without danger of failing, so long as they do it together.

Since the vast majority of financial transactions are made using cheques or credit transfers, only a small proportion of the total money supply circulates as notes and coins. However, in providing this token money the banks have to withdraw some of their cash reserve from the central bank, and this forms a limit to total bank lending. As the money supply rises, so too does the amount of notes and coins required by the commercial banks to supply to their customers. Thus their accounts with the central bank run down and they must curtail their lending.

Since the commercial banks make their profits on the money they supply, it is natural that they should want to supply as much as possible. The duty of the central bank is to control this supply by curbing in their enthusiasm.

The only way that the central bank can do this is by setting a minimum interest rate at which they can borrow money and lend to their customers. The 'punishment' for over-supplying money is, therefore, that the commercial banks are forced to charge more for the money they have already supplied. It's a nice business to be in - when you are in trouble, the government enforces a price rise in the product you supply. The cost of over-supplying money is thus borne by the borrowers.

The banks are the great anomaly in our economic system. The theory is that banks are supposed to be part of the competitive commercial system.

Yet, by enforcing a minimum interest rate, the government via the central bank effectively prevents them from competing. The excuse is that a commercial bank cannot be allowed to fail because it would disrupt the whole economy. This is true, but it only reinforces the argument that banks should not be part of the competitive system, and that the banking system is in urgent need of reform.

The Business Cycle

In analysing the activities of the banking system, it is not too much of a simplification to consider the whole banking system as a single bank. Since the banks tend to co-ordinate their lending policies and the central bank fixes the price (interest rate) at which they trade, the individual banks act effectively as branches of one large bank.

To simplify matters even more, we can consider this single, large bank to be supplying money to an economy which has no money of its own. Thus, the bank must supply money in order for the economy to work. Much of this money goes to companies in order for them to create goods and services, and to private individuals to help them to buy these goods and services. We can call this part of the system the 'working economy'.

In addition, the bank also lends to companies and individuals to buy assets. It is the link between the working economy and the asset markets which is the main cause of the phenomenon known as the business cycle, which is really a credit cycle, or a banking cycle.

The money that is lent to the working economy may circulate there without either increasing or decreasing so long as there is no 'leakage' to or from the asset market. The bank makes profits from its loans via the interest paid. If it uses all this money to pay its employees and its shareholders then the money in the working economy stays the same. If it keeps back some profit, then money is withdrawn from the working economy. Since any profit retained is an increase in reserves they can also be used as a basis for further lending. Thus the bank can increase or decrease the money supply to the working economy as it wishes.

The money that circulates in the working economy is the economy's working capital and is more or less proportional to the level of economic activity. Thus, keeping this constant helps to maintain the working economy at its current level, increasing it helps to stimulate growth, and reducing it causes a slow down. If the bank did not also lend to the asset markets then regulating the economy would not be difficult. All that would be required is for the bank to increase its lending at a rate equal to the expected economic growth.

Unfortunately, the bank lends to companies and individuals so that they can buy assets, and this happens predominantly when the working economy is growing. In addition, companies and individuals may save from their profits and wages to buy assets, so that money also flows from the working economy to the asset markets. When the economy stops or slows down, assets are sold off, loans are called in, and savings are held as money. The result is a flow of money from the asset markets and the working economy back to the bank.

Thus, there are three phases of money flow in the banking cycle. First, money flows from the bank to the working economy. Secondly, money flows from the bank and the working economy to the asset markets. Finally, money flows from the asset markets and the working economy back to the bank. In the first phase, business is booming and the working economy grows. In the second phase, companies and individuals buy assets, and their prices rise. In the third phase, the working economy slows down, asset prices fall as business, and individuals sell.

It would be ideal if the first and second phases could be prolonged indefinitely. However, this is impossible because the working economy is not a single business but a complex mixture of different enterprises. Some will succeed and some will fail. As the first phase proceeds, the successful companies will repay their loans, and the less successful ones will borrow more. Eventually, during the second phase, some companies will begin to fail, and the bank will take over their collateral assets. In selling off these assets, the bank precipitates the third phase, in which asset prices fall and money flows back to the bank.

This third and final phase is particularly vicious. When asset prices fall, so does the value of the collateral assets pledged against the bank's loans. The value of some of these assets will fall below the corresponding loan value and the bank will call in the loan. This causes a flow of money from the working economy back to the bank, and it is this that slows down an already faltering economy.

In addition, business failures are contagious. When a business fails, all its creditors lose money, and this could be enough to cause some of them to fail also. In the worst case, there is a domino effect and large sections of commerce may collapse in succession.

The only business in this scheme of things that is in no danger of failing is the bank itself. In the above analysis, we have assumed that the bank was a passive actor in the drama. In real life, the banks are also active in buying and selling assets to make profits. Since they also run many of the asset markets, they are in a good position to make higher than average gains. In addition, they have no obligation to ensure that the working economy runs smoothly, in fact, since the banking cycle is profitable for them, they have a vested interest in precipitating the final phase.

The banking cycle is as severe as ever it was and the central bank even less influential than in the days of gold. The only sure things in all this chaos are banking profits and the impossibility of bank failure. The moral for the wise investor is that banks are a very good long-term investment, even though booms and busts will be with us for the foreseeable future.

Chapter Ten

A Wider, Deeper, Longer Term View

The Working Economy

In the working economy of a modern industrial state, companies borrow money from the banks so that they can either expand their operations or pay for losses that otherwise would put them out of business. Most of this money goes into providing employment, either at the company itself, or for those who supply the company with the things that it needs to operate.

Activity in the working economy takes place via the markets for goods and services, whereby consumers pass on money to the companies; and employment in which companies return money to their employees. The companies also pay part of their income to shareholders as dividends. Of the money paid by companies to employees and shareholders, most is spent on goods and services. However, some is saved and is thereby taken out of the working economy. More money leaves the working economy when companies put money into reserve accounts, use it to pay interest, or to repay their bank loans. This loss may be partly compensated, or over compensated, by new bank lending to both companies and individuals. The system will be stable so long as there is enough money in circulation to facilitate all the transactions which are necessary to sustain it.

Given this analysis, it might seem an easy task to keep the economy running at a steady, even pace, simply by regulating the money supply to the working economy. However, the commercial banks are public companies, and they have a duty to their shareholders to maximise profits. Economic stability is not their responsibility, and since bank profits depend on the total amount of money supplied, their self interest is to increase it as much as possible. Thus, there is a natural tendency for the banks to push the economy to grow as fast as it can, and to inflate when it cannot. However, in certain circumstances, the banks are obliged to shrink the money supply, and this causes the economy to shrink.

Company failure

One natural reason for the working economy to slow down is simply that some companies will fail. The competition in industry and commerce ensures that there are losers as well as winners. Company failure puts people out of work and their wages are no longer available to buy goods and services. If company start-ups take place at the same rate as company failures, then the situation is contained and the working economy can remain stable.

However, when a company fails, it frequently leaves money owing to other companies, and this can cause problems if the creditor companies are unable to absorb the losses. So there is a tendency for one failure to provoke other failures. This process does not propagate very far since there are usually many more successful companies than unsuccessful ones. This is not a bad thing. It is necessary for weak companies to fail so that their assets can be recycled by stronger companies.

A further problem arises in the way this redistribution of assets takes place. When a company fails, it is usual for the bank to take charge of the company's assets. In selling off these assets, the bank may depress the price of similar assets. This puts other collateral assets in jeopardy, and the bank may have to call in other loans. This process can be vicious, and a downward spiral may take hold.

It seems likely, that without the linkage to the asset market, the working economy would be able to continue at high employment indefinitely. Of course, companies would still fail, and banks would still take over their collateral assets. However, this would proceed at a steady rate, and as old businesses became defunct, new ones would take their place.

Assets and Asset Markets

The market for assets can be viewed as separate from the working economy, though linked to it in several ways. Assets are simply those things which we own without consuming. A house is an asset, a car is a consumer good, even though some cars are more expensive than some houses. We buy assets, not to consume them, but to obtain some kind of benefit from their ownership. They are bought and sold on markets, but unlike the market for goods and services, higher prices do not generally bring forth increased supply, which in the short and medium term, is fixed. Asset markets are essential so that assets can be redistributed according to need. When a bank takes over the collateral assets of a failed company, it can sell them on the asset markets. The money the bank receives from these sales pays the losses of the company, and is equivalent to the loan being repaid. Both saving and the proceeds from asset sales go to the banks, and represent money taken out of the working economy. In addition, investors buy assets as a way of storing the value of money they do not wish to spend.

The working economy therefore needs the asset market as a way of storing the value of savings and to recycle the assets of failed companies. The idea that the asset markets form the main way in which savings are channelled into investment, is simply not true. Real investment, that is, the construction of new manufacturing equipment and new facilities for living, takes place within the working economy. The asset markets deal almost exclusively with assets which already exist, they are, essentially, second hand markets.

The two important participants in the asset markets are banks wishing to sell off collateral assets, and companies wishing to buy them. Investors also participate to trade assets as a means of storing value of savings. However, there is another class of participants in the asset markets whose business is less essential. There are the speculators, who buy and sell to make profits from short term trading. It is the actions of the speculators which provides the destabilising effect, and causes much of the market volatility.

Speculation in the Asset Markets

The weakness of the economic system is that asset markets are driven mainly by speculation, and consequently they do not establish a price level corresponding to the real supply and demand for assets. The theory of a market is that real buyers and sellers should establish equilibrium of supply and demand based on price level. Speculation disrupts this process.

Speculators react to changes in price rather than actual price level. Thus, they will not buy when prices are low, but when prices are rising, they will sell, not when prices are high, but when they are falling. They buy, not because they want to use the assets, but because they expect others to buy the assets from them at a higher price. They sell, not because they no longer need the assets, but because they see no prospect of obtaining any more profit. Thus, speculation heightens market highs and deepens market lows.

On a small scale, speculation would not be too harmful. The problem arises because banks are willing to lend for this purpose, and they lend in massive amounts. The natural highs of market price are considerably enhanced by speculators buying on margin, and the lows are considerably deepened by speculators selling off to repay their loans, and selling short to make further profits.

However, speculation is not the prime cause of fluctuations in the level of economic activity. This results from the uncontrolled nature of money supply to the working economy. The effect of speculation is to exacerbate these fluctuations by anticipating them. Thus, booms and busts in the working economy are enhanced, and the stable conditions needed for steady growth are never sustained for any length of time.

Limits to Boom and Bust

In system theory, a situation in which the changes are self-reinforcing, is known as positive feedback. It means simply that the system's internal mechanism will reinforce any change of state. If changes are up then the system favours upward change, if changes are down then the system favours downward change. Theoretically, zero change would favour stability, but this equilibrium is unstable, and any slight fluctuation will initiate self reinforcing change, either up or down.

In our economy, because the money supply is uncontrolled, the system is inherently unstable. Without other factors to limit the swings, the economy would slowly bloom into rampant inflation or collapse into deepest recession. The Central Bank influences money supply by changes in interest rates. However, this is too indirect and too delayed to provide the tight control necessary to establish the money supply level at the desired level.

The natural tendency of the system is to go to extremes. The money supply naturally increases or decreases, either boom or bust, and switching interest rates simply switches the system from one trend to the other. There is no level of interest rate that can make the system stable.

When money floods into the working economy, the markets which supply goods and services experience a rise in demand. This may not cause a significant rise in prices if companies can increase supply without increasing their per-unit production costs. This is possible if they can readily find unemployed workers. However, when full employment is approached, employers have to bid up wages in order to tempt employees from other companies. Once this happens, those already in employment will need pay rises to discourage them changing jobs, and wage inflation begins.

Since more money is now being paid to a constant number of workers, the result is not an increase in production, but a rise in its wages. This propagates from wages to the price of goods, and services. More money coming into the system after it reaches full employment simply causes price inflation. The limiting tendency of economic activity in a boom situation is accelerating inflation. The central bank can prevent full employment being reached by raising interest rates, which, to be effective must cause economic activity to contract.

When the working economy is shrinking, companies cut back on production, workers are laid off, and prices of goods and services fall. Wages are generally lower so that people have less to spend and the economy shrinks further. Logically, the natural lower limit for economic activity should be zero employment. This would be the case if all citizens were employees or did not have significant savings. However, the rich are always with us - there are always people who have some money, either saved or invested, who will not accept starvation. There will always exist enough basic demand for economic activity to bottom out well before it reaches zero. Part of this is government spending which will not fall to zero. For these reasons, the working economy does not entirely collapse. Once asset prices have reached their low point, banks will begin to lend again, if not to companies then to speculators.

In fact, by this stage of the cycle, few companies will want to borrow anyway. They have had to cut production because of the fall in demand, and this usually means laying off workers and getting rid of surplus plant and equipment. Other companies will have gone out of business. Therefore, interest rates have to fall significantly in order to tempt borrowers back into debt.

In the boom, banks can force borrowers to repay loans, but in the recession, they cannot force them to borrow. Thus, the fall into recession is always quicker than the rise to recovery. In fact, recovery can only begin if the money supply is increased to support capital formation and/or increased production of goods and services. Extra money supplied to buy assets simply drives up their price and has no effect on the working economy.

The modern custom of paying money to unemployed workers ensures that recessions are not as severe as they used to be. The fall in employment does not cause a proportional fall in demand because the unemployed are no longer without money to buy essential goods and services. Since the unemployed are not desperate, this also means that wage levels do not fall significantly, and this also helps to maintain demand. The theorists of capitalism express great regret at this government 'interference' in the free market. However, a look at the past will convince us that raw capitalism is as unappetising as raw meat.

The Great Depression

The worst recession of modern times was in the 1930s; it was so severe that it earned itself the name 'The Great Depression'. It began in the USA and Europe about 1929, and spread to the rest of the world as the world trade collapsed and the demand for raw materials fell away. It lasted nearly ten years. Unemployment approached 20% in Europe, and 25% in the USA. It blighted the lives of many young people who grew up without ever having had a job or even adequate nourishment.

During world war one, American and European industry experienced a huge increase in productivity. This was due to several factors, but chiefly an expanded work force, the use of machines, and new mass production methods. Unfortunately, the rewards of these increases were channelled almost entirely into profits. There were only small increases in rates of pay, and in some sectors pay actually fell. Thus while the productive capacity of the western nations increased rapidly, their ability to consume did not.

In Britain, workers were forced to accept a reduction in wages and this precipitated the General Strike. Meanwhile, legislation in the USA was directed against unions and minimum wages. The resulting surge in profits and their reinvestment in stocks and shares caused the five-year boom on the Wall Street stock market. Industry wanted both cheap labour to produce goods, and wealthy citizens to buy them. That they could not have both didn't seem obvious at the time. By 1929, industry was beginning to cut production as demand for its increased production failed to materialise.

In the USA, many small and medium sized banks failed. Profits fell, Wall Street crashed, and the Great Depression began.

The theory of capitalism says that recessions are necessary, and once market forces have come back into balance, the situation will move back towards full employment. So, at first, no one was inclined to do anything about the rising unemployment, since it was expected that it would cure itself. At the time, only one economist of any standing recognised what was happening. This was J M Keynes. He realised that the fall off in demand would not necessarily correct itself as the theory suggested.

He showed that the economy could stick with high unemployment for a long time because supply exceeded demand by such a large factor. In this extreme case, market forces required 25% of the population to starve to death to bring labour supply into balance with demand. Low interest rates were not sufficient to pull the economy out of deep recession. People had money only for essentials, and because of increased productivity, these could be produced with a smaller work force than ever before.

The task was to find useful employment for the 'surplus' workers so that they could be paid wages and brought back into the working economy. Keynes's remedy was for the government to borrow large amounts of money and spend it on public works, like roads, harbours, drainage schemes, etc. This would have worked in two ways, directly by creating employment, and indirectly by providing the traumatised banking system with a borrower of impeccable security.

After the experience of German hyperinflation in 1923, the banks were wary of government inspired economic solutions. The prudent instincts of the bankers prevailed, and Keynes's remedy was not applied with any thoroughness - at least in democratic countries. Autocratic regimes in Germany and Russia had no such inhibitions, and they both enjoyed full employment when the rest of the world was languishing in depression. During this period, Russia created its heavy industrial complexes, and Germany built its system of autobahns and re-equipped its armed forces.

Ironically, in the rest of Europe and the USA, unemployment only ended with the advent of the second world war, when governments were forced to borrow massively for the 'public work' of waging war.

Post War Inflation

During the second world war, the banking system in Europe and the USA responded to the emergency and provided all the money necessary to sustain the war effort. Inflation increased, but not as much as in the first war. Bankers found that even without a gold-backed money supply, inflation could be kept within reasonable bounds.

Since the war, governments have accepted it as their duty to control the level of economic activity so as to avoid the twin perils of rampant inflation and deep recession. Previously, this was left to the operation of capitalist markets. At first, during the post war reconstruction, inflation was not a problem; economic expansion was sufficient to soak up all the available money supply.

However, in the late sixties, inflation took hold, and the oil price shocks of the early seventies sent inflation to record levels. In the UK, the difficulty was compounded by the tendency for government to use interest rates as a political weapon. It is a well known that both political parties used them to create pre-election economic boom.

The Keynsian remedy for curing unemployment was used extensively for post war reconstruction. The government borrowed extensively for public works, and the subsequent inflation conveniently reduced the real value of these debts. The result was a period of high interest rates in anticipation of more inflation, even after inflation was down to single figures.

The latest stage of this unfolding economic drama has been the sell-off of the state owned industries built up during the post war years. The current idea is that government spending should not be greater than 50% of national spending. This might seem a sensible arrangement, but it is not working as well as it should because a vast amount of government spending is on social benefits.

In the past, the government reduced unemployment by spending on public works, which protected companies from the worst effects of falling demand. Now, the government just pays money to the jobless as unemployment benefit to achieve the same end. This takes up a large amount of government revenue, and means that not much is left for really necessary public works. It seems that government has lost confidence that it can carry out public works, and has accepted the idea that private companies should be able to build and operate any public facilities that are necessary. Meanwhile, the publicly owned infrastructure is crumbling because no one can think of a way of making it profitable for private companies to run it.

However, the post war years have seen the world trade system recover and expand to proportions never seen, even in the days of empire. This means that no national economy is independent, and is linked to other nations by its imports and exports, by capital flows, and by the effects of speculation on world asset markets. However, before we analyse the global economy, it is necessary to take a brief look at the foreign exchange system.

Foreign Currency Exchange

In ancient times, as money came into widespread use, merchants trading overseas were always prepared to accept payment for their goods in foreign money. Since the value of all money was based on its gold or silver content, as a last resort, the merchants could always melt down foreign coins into bullion, and re-mint it as their native currency. However, more often, merchants just exchanged gold and silver of one coinage for that of another on a proportional weight basis. This exchange was being done via money changers, who were also the first international bankers.

In medieval times, carrying large sums of gold and silver coins was a risky thing to do. Instead, merchants preferred to accept 'bills of exchange' in return for their goods, so long as they were drawn on a trustworthy bank.

A bill of exchange is simply an IOU, a combination of a bank note and a cheque. Instead of having to transport large quantities of coin back to his home port, the merchant could accept a bill of exchange. On his return, he could then present to his local bank and receive coins in his own currency. Similarly, instead of carrying large quantities of coin abroad, he could purchase bills of exchange in the currency he would be using.

The merchants used bills of exchange for trading, and the banks undertook the risk of transferring gold and silver coin from country to country. However, since the banks had customers from many countries, they only needed to transfer the net balance, and they could do this once or twice a year, or whenever it was convenient. In addition, in any one country, the bills were bought and sold between the banks, so that net settlements in coin were relatively small.

During their clearing operations, the banks in a particular country would establish exchange rates between different currencies. Since all money consisted of gold or silver coin, these rates of exchange fluctuated only within narrow limits. These were set by the need to melt down coins of currencies in excess supply and recoin them as coins of currencies in excess demand.

From these small beginnings, foreign exchange markets and international finance were born. In the heyday of the British Empire, world trade flourished using the British pound as the preferred currency. This was possible because early in the eighteenth century, Britain established the pound on a gold standard, permitting coin to be melted down and shipped as bullion when necessary. This gave other countries the confidence to accept bills of exchange in pounds with the knowledge that, if necessary, they could redeem them for gold at the Bank of England.

As London became the centre for world trade, so it became the centre for trade finance, and foreign exchange. For those countries with gold and silver coinage, the exchange rates were more or less fixed. For countries with paper money, the exchange rate was fixed on the basis of supply and demand against gold.

After the first world war, the world trade system, centred on London, began to disintegrate. Britain simply did not have enough gold to keep the system running. By 1931, the demand for payments in gold was so strong that a huge rise in interest rates would have been necessary to stop it. Effectively, the world lost confidence in paper pounds and preferred to have gold instead. Since the UK was in recession, the government took the wise decision to abandon the gold standard. After that, trade between Europe and the rest of the world declined as the world slipped into the Great Depression.

After world war two, the Bretton woods' agreement created a managed system of exchange rates. This required each country to fix its exchange rate against the dollar which itself was fixed against gold. This worked reasonably well until 1971 when the USA abandoned the gold standard. In 1973 most currencies 'floated', that is, allowed their exchange rate to be established by supply and demand on the foreign exchange markets. This is the system now in place today.

The Foreign Exchange Market is not located in any one place, but is simply a service provided by banks in the major financial centres throughout the world. Of course, with modern electronic communication, any slight price differences in exchange rates between different financial centres are instantly removed. Thus, the exchange rates quoted in New York, Tokyo, Frankfurt, are the same as those in London.

Foreign Exchange Barter

This world market in currencies is not easy to understand. In the days of gold, all currencies could be valued in terms of a certain weight of gold. Now, money is flexible, and the value of each currency varies according to the conditions in its native economy. There is now no absolute money against which every currency can be valued. Therefore, instead of the world's ten major currencies having ten valuations against gold, there are 45 cross exchange rates, each dependent on the supply and demand situation between each pair of currencies.

Because the thing traded is money, and since money is used in payment, it is impossible to say who is the buyer and who the seller. If I exchange British pounds for American dollars, it is clear to me that I am buying dollars. However, the American counter-party to the trade knows that he is buying pounds. We each feel ourselves to be the buyer and the other the seller, and we are both correct from the standpoint of out native currency. However, the absolute truth of the matter is that we are bartering currency - my pounds for his dollars.

After nearly three thousand years of trade using money based on precious metals, the system has now regressed to barter. Of course, the goods and services traded are paid for in money, but the money itself is exchanged in a barter system. Exporters have no fixed price at which they can export goods, and importers have no fixed price at which they can import goods. They must rely on the barter system of the currency markets.

Exchange rates depend on supply and demand for the various currencies, which in the long term are based on export/import values. For this purpose, exchange rates tend to be self-balancing. If a country experiences inflation of its internal prices, foreign goods appear cheaper and its own goods become more expensive to foreigners. Thus imports increase and exports decrease. This gives rise to an extra demand for foreign currency and its exchange rate tends to decline. This is a self-correcting process that tends to bring exchange rates into economic balance.

If currency movements were only for the purposes of trade, then exchange rates would be steady and stable though not fixed. However, other businesses use foreign currency, and these account for almost all the money passing through the foreign exchange market. The total value of foreign exchange business transacted on the international markets, in a typical day, is approximately $1000 billion.

To make sure that you do not mistake this number, here it is again written out in full, it is $1,000,000,000,000 per DAY. Trade accounts for only a tiny fraction of this enormous amount. The rest is for businesses which require the buying and selling of foreign currencies. Investment in foreign assets is one such business, but even this cannot account for such a huge traffic in currencies. It would seem that the major part of foreign exchange business is done for the purpose of speculation.

Foreign Investment

Investment funds, investing steadily in foreign assets, need to buy them with the relevant currency, and to obtain it they must bid up the exchange rate for that currency. As the exchange rate rises, their earlier investments appear more valuable, and the assets of that country become even more attractive. On the other hand, when an investment fund sells off its assets in a country, it needs also to sell the foreign currency. Thus, as it sells some unprofitable foreign assets the others become less and less attractive as the exchange rate falls. This process is clearly unstable.

Banks also add to this effect when they lend to foreign companies. This is, after all, an investment in foreign assets. Even if they lend in their own currency, the borrowers must exchange the money before they can use it domestically. Thus the currency rises, the assets appear to rise in value and the loans appear profitable. When loans and interest are repaid, the currency falls and the loans appear to be failing and the banks call in other loans.

Foreign investment is a positive feedback situation, and is a cause of instability in world exchange rates. The recent violent falls in Asian currencies were triggered by this process. In this case, it was mainly banks lending to Asian companies which pushed up the exchange rates. However, as soon as the lending stopped and the interest had to be paid, the loans became less attractive, and when the banks began to ask for repayment, the currencies collapsed.

In addition to this natural instability, the activity of speculators increases exchange rate fluctuations. Again, banks lend money for this purpose and also indulge in it themselves. The world bank and the international monetary fund have the task of trying to stabilise this situation, acting, as it were, as world central bankers.

It is also in the interests of each individual country to stabilise its own exchange rate. This task falls to the central bank. Just as central banks try to avoid booms and busts in their own economy, they also try to prevent wild swings in their exchange rates. For this task, they have the usual mechanism of interest rates, and in addition, they can buy and sell currency on the foreign exchange market. The tendency is for them to use the interest rate for longer-term control and 'intervention' in the foreign exchange market to smooth out short-term changes in the exchange rate.

The swings in economic activity within our national economic system call forth higher, then lower, bank interest rates. These swings cause changes in the exchange rate. Foreign funds, seeking higher yields on their cash, buy the pound when interest rates are high. Then, when they fall, they move to some other high yielding currency. Thus, high interest rates, which are designed to reduce the domestic money supply, also attract foreign funds which effectively increase the money supply. Likewise, low interest rates which are designed to increase money supply also encourage money to flow abroad thus reducing the money supply. This is one of the mechanisms that link national economies to the global system.

International Lending

All that has been said above about economic instability is inherent in the way in which banks are licensed to lend money. Within any one country, the central bank can always force the banking system to put up interest rates, and eventually this may reduce the money supply.

In international lending, the World Bank and the International Monetary Fund act as Central Bankers, but they cannot enforce interest rates. Instead, they try to stop the system of world currencies going unstable by providing back-up credit. The 'run' on a country's currency is rather like a run on a bank. It is a temporary panic by holders of the currency, who perceive that its value may fall. By rushing to get out they may help to precipitate a collapse. The money that is loaned to countries with exchange rate difficulties at cheap interest rates simply tides them over the crisis. It does nothing to remove the inherent causes of the crisis, and its cost falls on the world's governments.

The international lending system is inherently unstable for exactly the same reason that national credit systems are unstable, money supply is uncontrolled.

In addition, there is the added instability of the exchange rate system. The practice of speculation, encouraged by the banking system, adds considerably to the swings in exchange rates and hence interest rates. Consequently, foreign exchange markets are extremely volatile, and are becoming more so as larger and larger amounts of money are shunted from one currency to another in order to create profit or avoid loss.

Trouble Ahead

It is always foolish to make predictions of doom. Unsuccessful prophets are not respected in any country. Successful ones are usually charged with rocking the boat, and may even be blamed for the capsize when it finally occurs. However, the instability of the world financial system is too obvious to be ignored. It seems inevitable that the system will collapse unless it is changed, but exactly when and how it will fail, is not at all clear.

It may be asked, if this instability is so obvious, why is no one doing anything about it. The answer is that those who understand what is going on are the very ones who cannot afford to stop it. They are the international bankers and fund managers whose profits rely on the volatility of asset markets, both nationally and internationally.

George Soros has warned of this danger, first in 1985 in his book, and since then in public speeches. As a speculator of impeccable timing, he is very much aware of the mechanisms that send markets rushing from boom to bust and back again. He is also aware that these cycles are deepening, and that at some point, there will be major bank failures.

Already, Barings bank has gone out of existence due to excessive losses in futures trading. The managers escaped prosecution by claiming that they did not know what was happening. It seems like a weak excuse, but we can easily believe it. In the Great Depression, the bankers didn't know what was happening, and the system is now much more complicated than it was then. In the past 100 years the fundamental basis of banking has changed, money is no longer based on gold. The banking system is now based on confidence and trust, and these can disappear even more quickly than gold.

The managers of international banks and investment funds are in the same situation as the operators who ran the Chernobyl Nuclear Reactor. These engineers knew their plant was unstable, but the pressure to squeeze just a little more power out of it was a challenge to their ingenuity. They took it to the edge several times before it finally went out of control. Similarly, the pressure to squeeze just a little more profit out of the foreign exchange markets will probably take us to the limit of stability several times before the final meltdown.

The Coming Crash

Hopefully, the world system of trade and finance will continue to operate successfully until we have all retired and put our savings into government bonds of utmost security. When the crash comes, it will bring a huge disruption to domestic economies in proportion to their dependence on imports and exports and this looks bad for Britain, which is traditionally dependent on trade. However, we may escape the worst if, by then, we have joined the European Common Currency. Then at least our exports and imports to Europe will be exempt from exchange rate variations.

The creation of a European economic super-state, with 350 million people and a common currency, will provide the UK with a haven from a world financial crash. However, it will make life harder for other countries in the world. In particular, Japan and USA will both find themselves pushed down the league table of reserve currencies. The adjustment of the world economic system to the new Europe may be the event that shocks the exchange rate system into collapse.

A major problem for the US economy, is the huge amount of dollar securities held by central banks around the world. In the coming years, foreign central banks will want to exchange at least some of these for European securities. It is likely that the Europe currency will become the world's reserve currency in place of the dollar.

As dollar securities are sold off, the dollar will fall, and once this begins, speculation will ensure that the process accelerates. The managers of the US domestic economy will have two options. The first alternative will be to increase interest rates to discourage foreign owners of dollars selling them. The second will be to encourage inflation with low interest rates in order to devalue the foreign debt before it can be redeemed. Given the self-reinforcing tendencies of both asset price changes and foreign exchange markets, and the activities of speculators, neither of these options will be possible without some kind of crash

A problem for the Japanese economy is that their pension funds hold a vast amount of US government bonds. Over the past twenty years, as the Japanese have been exporting their way to prosperity, the money they have earned has been largely invested abroad. Because of this, the exchange rate has not adjusted upwards as it should have done in consequence of its huge export surplus. The older generation of Japanese savers who created this wealth will eventually retire and want to cash in their savings. Once these funds begin to repatriate their foreign investments, the Yen will begin to rise. This will make these foreign assets less attractive, the process of withdrawal will accelerate, and the Yen exchange rates will go even higher.

Happy Endings

After 1914, the world economies were forced to abandon gold as the basis for both domestic money supply and international trade and finance. At that time, there was an opportunity to put in place a system of regulating money supply directly to make economic conditions stable. However, this was not done, and now there is a great risk of financial disruption in world trade and domestic economies more serious than that experienced in the Great Depression.

Eventually, governments will have to take control of money supply directly and it will fall to the coming generations to put things right. Meanwhile, we hope to be able to retire and take income from our investments. It seems unlikely that any disturbance to the world economy will force the UK government to repudiate its obligations to holders of its bonds. Hopefully, we will be able to sell our growth stocks and buy bonds before asset markets crash to any significant extent. It is unlikely that pension funds will escape a crash, they are too big and too slow. Our own small funds do stand a good chance of escaping a crash if we sell out soon enough.

Since 1700, an income from British Government bonds has been the basis of a happy retirement for many citizens, and looking into the future, it would appear that this will continue. The government will pay the interest on these bonds out of taxes, and these taxes will be paid by the working population, which will include our sons and daughters. Thus, the next generation will look after its elders, as it always has done, and always will do. There is simply no other way.

Investing in Options: For the Private Investor

A hardback book which shows you exactly how to 'gear' your money to provide more growth. Step-by-step it teaches how you appraise an options position, looking at the rewards and risks, and then how to execute a deal. There are plenty of examples to show you exactly how its done and how to trade profitably.

For the experienced options buyer there are examples of option combinations which can be used to create almost any desired outcome. With options you can make money whichever direction the market is moving.

128 pages   1-873668-59-7   £14.95   Hardback

Successful Spread betting

Spread Betting offers investors a simple and direct way of dealing in the world's financial markets and has significant advantages over other methods of dealing: ...It gives you access to financial markets in which you couldn't normally deal without being a registered broker, for example foreign exchange ...Any money you make from Spread Betting is Tax Free ...You can also bet on events and outcomes in the sporting world ...There are no dealing charges - no brokerage or commission fees ...Spread Betting firms offer instant dealing and extended hours so you can take out a position even when the underlying markets are closed.

160 pages   ISBN:1-873668-58-9   £12.95

Investing on the Internet

The Internet is revolutionising the way ordinary investors are going about increasing their personal wealth. For the first time everyone can now access information that used to be available only to the investment professionals. And with *Investing on the Internet*, you can be at the forefront of this transformation.

This handy guide will lead you to the best investment tools there are on the web, almost all of which are completely free. Full site addresses are given with a review of content, speed and usefulness.

192 pages   ISBN:1-873668-73-2   £4.95

International Dictionary of Personal Finance

This dictionary provides a basic vocabulary of terms used in the world of personal finance, from 'A' shares to zero-rating and from accelerated depreciation to yield. Words used in all areas of finance are covered, not just those from basic investment, but also from the arenas of banking, law, national insurance and tax. Both British and American usages are included.

128 pages   ISBN:1-873668-54-6   £6.95

Understand Shares in a Day Second Edition

Shows how the share market really works. Inexperienced investors will learn: ❑ About different types of shares ... ❑ Why share prices fluctuate... ❑ How to read the financial pages ... ❑ How shares are bought and sold ... ❑ How risk can be spread with investment and unit trusts ... ❑ How to build a portfolio of shares ...❑ The risks and rewards of Penny Shares

Once this groundwork has been covered, the book explores more complex ideas which will appeal to both beginners and experienced investors alike.

128 pages   *ISBN:1-873668-73-2 £6.95*

Understand Bonds & Gilts in a Day 2nd Edition

This handy title shows potential investors, and those with an interest in the bond markets, how to assess the potential risks and rewards, giving a simple to follow set of criteria on which to base investment decisions. It also teaches even the most arithmetically shy how to calculate the yield on a bond and plan an income based portfolio. The confusing terminology used in the bond market is clearly explained with working definitions of many terms and a comprehensive glossary.

112 pages   *ISBN:1-873668-72-4 £6.95*

To order any of these books, please order on the world wide web at <u>www.takethat.co.uk</u> or complete the form below or use a plain piece of paper and send to:

Europe/Asia TTL, PO Box 200, Harrogate HG1 2YR, England (or fax to 01423-526035, or email: sales@net-works.co.uk).

USA/Canada Trafalgar Square, PO Box 257, Howe Hill Road, North Pomfret, Vermont 05053 (or fax to 802-457-1913, call toll free 800-423-4525, or email: tsquare@sover.net)

Postage and handling charge:
UK - £1 for first book, and 50p for each additional book. USA - $5 for first book, and $2 for each additional book (all shipments by UPS, please provide street address). Elsewhere - £3 for first book, and £1.50 for each additional book via surface post (for airmail and courier rates, please fax or email for a price quote)

Book	Qty	Price

❑ I enclose payment for _____

❑ Please debit my Visa/Amex/Mastercard No:

Postage

Total:

Expiry date: ▢▢▢▢   Signature:

Name: _____

Address: _____

_____

Postcode/Zip: _____

Lterm